Sara Payne

A Mother's Story

Sara Payne

A Mother's Story

Sara Payne
with Anna Gekoski

Hodder & Stoughton
LONDON SYDNEY AUCKLAND

First published in Great Britain in 2004
This paperback edition 2005

10 9 8 7 6 5 4

British Library Cataloguing in Publication Data
A record for this book is available from the British Library

ISBN 0 340 86278 5

Printed and bound in Great Britain by
Clays Ltd, St Ives plc

Typeset in Goudy by Avon DataSet Ltd,
Bidford on Avon, Warwickshire

The paper and board used in this paperback are natural
recyclable products made from wood grown in sustainable forests.
The manufacturing processes conform to the environmental regulations
of the country of origin.

Hodder & Stoughton
A Division of Hodder Headline Ltd
338 Euston Road
London NW1 3BH
www.madaboutbooks.com

To my mum Elizabeth, for making me who I am.

Contents

1

SARAH

Mike and I were childhood sweethearts. We met at the tender age of sixteen, both just out of school with a handful of CSEs between us, and our whole lives in front of us. We were from similar backgrounds – big, working-class families from Walton-on-Thames in Surrey – and our expectations of life were limited to what we knew. Further education was for those with money and, although we weren't badly off, it was a luxury we couldn't afford and didn't expect. It was assumed that we would go out and get a job and that's what we both did. I started work in a chemist's, while Mike did shifts at a local factory, and we both felt very grown up, bringing a wage packet home every week. After several months of friendship, we officially got together on 9 November 1985, a few days before Mike's seventeenth birthday. We really connected straight away, spending hours talking about anything and everything. Mike was funny, gentle and kind, quite unlike the other boys I had been out with. I thought I'd found my soul mate.

Within months I was pregnant. It certainly wasn't planned –

as we were still kids ourselves – but there was never any question of us not having the child. We were from big families who celebrated birth, and being pregnant was something to be proud of. But before we could tell our families the happy news, I suffered a miscarriage. Although it was a shock, it was only a few weeks into the pregnancy and I have always been a firm believer in letting nature take its course. That baby was obviously not meant for this world. Within a matter of months I was expecting again and, after waiting an appropriate time, we made the announcement. At first our parents were slightly concerned about our age, but they could see that our relationship was loving and strong and we were obviously in it for the long term, so they supported our decision and told us we would be wonderful parents.

Sadly, just as Mike and I were starting a family of our own, mine broke up, when my parents Brian and Elizabeth separated. I was still in the early stages of my pregnancy when my mum announced that she was moving to Clacton, and Mike and I decided to go with her. After leafy Walton, we found it a dismal place and there was no decent work to be had, so we both ended up working in a convalescent home, me in the kitchen and Mike doing cleaning and odd jobs. Being around ill people all day depressed us and after a few months we decided to move back home. Back in Walton, we put our names on the council housing list and moved in with my dad, who was a lock-keeper and had a big house right on the Thames.

Our first baby, Lee, was born just after my eighteenth birthday and, although we were young, we adored being parents and it wasn't long before I was expecting once more. Sadly, I suffered another early miscarriage, but fell pregnant again soon afterwards. Luke was born eighteen months after Lee and a month later the council finally gave us a flat of our own in Walton.

It had all happened so fast. One minute I had just left school and had so many choices and so few responsibilities. Now, at the age of twenty, I had met my life partner, had two miscarriages, two children, moved three times in as many years, and had a house to run. We had both been forced to grow up very quickly. Always one to take his responsibilities seriously, Mike decided that he should think about a job with a future. His mum and dad were both in the off-licence business – with his mother Les managing a shop and his father Terry working as a trouble-shooter turning around the profits of businesses that were failing. Mike decided to follow in his parents' footsteps and got a job in a local off-licence, where he quickly moved up the ranks to deputy manager. He was soon offered a job at a shop in Goring in Sussex, with a spacious two-bedroom flat to go with it, so we packed our bags and moved once again. But, as had become our pattern, we weren't settled for long as Mike was offered a manager's job just after his twenty-first birthday. It was great news, but it meant another move, this time to East Preston in Sussex, where his parents now lived, and we moved in above Mike's new shop.

The next year, on 4 August 1990, we decided to get married. It was something that we had discussed dozens of times, but we didn't want to do it just because we had children. We wanted to wait until the time was right. The boys were a bit older now, we had a regular wage coming in, a home of our own and, most importantly, after five years together we couldn't imagine life without each other. It seemed the perfect time to tie the knot. Although neither of us was religious, we wanted to do things properly, so we had a traditional white wedding at East Preston church. I wore a long white dress, there were bridesmaids, flowers, and photos on the steps. As I said the words 'I do' I had no doubt that Mike and I would be together for ever. Afterwards we had a massive reception in a local pub with all our family and friends. We didn't have enough money for a honeymoon, but we had a lovely night in a local hotel.

Everything should have been perfect, but things took a turn for the worse shortly after we got married. Mike started falling into black moods whereby he would withdraw into himself for days on end, causing him to take time off work. He would say to me that some days it felt as if he were looking at the world through dark glasses. There was nothing wrong that he could pinpoint, it was just a general feeling that overtook him and he was unable to shake off. Then, as suddenly as it had come on, it was gone, and Mike would be laughing and joking as if it hadn't happened. We were young and knew nothing about mental illness, so we struggled on through the down times as best we could, putting them down to the pressures of working hard and having a young family to support. I loved Mike and just tried to accept the black times as part of who he was.

When I found out I was pregnant yet again, our happiness at the news was slightly marred by Mike's fluctuating moods. We sat down and talked over the implications of having a new baby, and decided that three children and the responsibility of managing a shop might prove too much. So Mike handed in his notice and we moved back home to Surrey where we had more family support. Until we found a place of our own, the boys and I lived with my mum, who had moved back from Clacton and now lived in Hersham, the village next to Walton. It was only a little bed-sit and there wasn't room for Mike too, so he stayed with his brother and got a job working nights at a petrol station, which he found much less stressful than managing the shop.

When we eventually managed to get some money together we rented a little house which was down the road from my mum. It was tiny, with one bedroom for Mike and me, a box room for the boys upstairs, and a tiny lounge and kitchen downstairs. It was always noisy and messy, full of children's laughter and tears, with toys and McDonalds' wrappers underfoot. But it was our home and, for the most part, we were happy.

Things improved for a time, but even with a less stressful lifestyle Mike's dark moods soon returned, and they lasted longer and longer each time. He would sit in his chair in the front room for hours not saying a word, hardly aware of what was going on around him. Finally we decided that he should see the doctor who diagnosed him as suffering from manic depression. When we asked how and why he had got it, the doctor said that it could be triggered by a nasty virus, which Mike had suffered several of in adult life, including chicken pox and inner ear infections. This gave us hope that the condition was temporary and the doctor gave him antidepressants to control the moods in the meantime. Mike started taking the pills and he quickly became himself again. He put on weight, was able to deal with the stresses and strains of life, and regained his confidence. It made a big difference to the quality of our family life.

Our third child, Sarah Evelyn Isobel Payne, made her grand entrance into the world on 13 October 1991, with a tuft of dark hair on her head and a tooth in her mouth. Just like Lee and Luke, Sarah arrived ten days later than expected. It was typical of our family, who are always late, but knowing Sarah's sweet nature I'm sure she felt bad about keeping me waiting. My labour started at midnight, with Mike out working the late shift at the petrol station, and the boys fast asleep, lying top to toe in the single bed they shared. I had just taken a relaxing hot bath and I collapsed on to the double bed with a sigh, looking forward to a good night's sleep. It was not to be. As my eyes fell on the cot beside the bed, ready for the new arrival, a vice-like pain suddenly clenched my stomach. I gasped and automatically put my hand to my belly, but as soon as the pain had come, it was gone again and, having been through this twice before, I knew that one twinge didn't necessarily mean that the baby was coming. So I calmly lay down, turned off the light, and closed my eyes. Just as sleep was coming over me the pain returned, more insistent than the last time. The clock glowed 12.30 a.m., half an hour after my last twinge. I knew this was it: 'Oh bugger,' I said aloud.

At that moment I sorely wished that I had listened to my mum when she had nagged us to get a telephone installed. But Mike and I, as usual, simply hadn't got round to it. Mike was not due home until the early hours, and I didn't know any of the neighbours yet, so I decided to go to Mum's, where I could leave the boys and call a taxi to the hospital. Gingerly getting out of bed, I padded next door into the boys' bedroom. I gently shook Lee, who at four years old was the eldest. 'Lee, we have to get up now, the baby's coming. We're going over to Granny's,' I told him. My waters chose that minute to break, and I knew we didn't have too much time to spare. Seeing my panic, Lee immediately took charge of the situation. 'It's OK, Mummy, I'll wake Luke,' he said, which was no mean feat as Luke was always difficult to get out of bed. But Lee managed it that night, explaining to his three-year-old brother that Mummy had to go to the hospital. Lee efficiently dressed them both before packing a bag with their pyjamas. He even remembered to put in Luke's safety blanket, a quilt with a blue frill, which he couldn't bear to be without. There was a last-minute panic to find Luke's shoes, and finally we were ready.

The walk to Mum's was only a short one, but it seemed to take for ever that night. We must have made a comical threesome. Lee insisted on carrying both my bag and theirs, as well as holding his brother's hand. Every so often I was forced to stop and sit down on the street, my hands clasped to my tummy, waiting for the worst of the contractions to pass. Lee would ask with concern, 'Are you all right, Mummy?', and I would assure him that I was fine until I was ready to carry on. When we finally arrived at Mum's it took several rings on the doorbell to rouse her, but as soon as she opened the door she knew what was happening. 'I told you to get a phone, you stupid girl,' she commented with a smile in her voice, and ushered us inside. Luke got straight in his granny's bed and went back to sleep, while Lee perched on the sofa and peered at me with concern.

The first thing I did was ring Mike at work. Alarmed to receive a call from me so late, he was immediately concerned.

'Are you all right, sweetheart?' he asked me.

I reassured him, 'I'm at Mum's, everything's fine, but the baby's coming. Can you meet me at the hospital?'

'I'm here on my own and I haven't got the keys to lock up,' he said, 'I'll call round and try to get someone to cover for me. Don't worry, I'll be there as soon as I can.'

'Wish me luck,' I said.

'Good luck. I love you.'

'You too.'

At that point we were quite calm. Mum had been through labour six times herself and I already had two children, so it was hardly a new experience. We knew that there were usually hours to spare between the first contractions and birth. But it soon became apparent that this time was different. Having waited so long, Sarah was now in a hurry. Mum had just picked up the phone to call a taxi, when I doubled over in pain, with a sharp intake of breath. It was only a few minutes since the last contraction and they were getting stronger all the time. The baby was coming – now – and there was no time to waste with taxis. 'Ring an ambulance,' I gasped. Mum rang 999, telling the reluctant operator that if they didn't hurry up the baby would be born on the carpet.

Waiting for the ambulance, I paced the room, doubling up in pain at regular intervals. Thankfully, it didn't take more than a few minutes to arrive and I was loaded into the back. I insisted that Mum and the boys stay at home, but as the ambulance doors shut I felt very alone. Mike had been with me through every stage of my first two labours, and I missed his reassuring presence.

We were halfway to the hospital when I was suddenly overtaken by the urge to push – I couldn't help myself. Seeing what was happening, the paramedic urged me, 'Try not to push. We're nearly there, just wait a little bit longer.'

'I can't stop it, I have to,' I cried, gripping his hand until it turned white.

'Pull over,' shouted the paramedic, and the ambulance swerved into a lay-by so they could check the progress of the baby.

'It's OK, I think we'll make it,' he told his colleague and the blue lights went on as we raced to the hospital.

We arrived at St Peter's in Chertsey at just gone 1.45 a.m. and I was put on a trolley. In the lift on the way up to the maternity ward I was consumed by the urge to start pushing again, but the nurse said, with alarm, 'No, no, no, not yet.' I was rushed into the delivery suite where there was no time to even check my blood pressure; it was all systems go. The relief was enormous as I was finally allowed to push, and at 2 a.m. Sarah was born.

'You've got a girl,' said the midwife, placing the little bundle on my stomach.

'A girl!' I exclaimed tearfully. Although a scan had revealed earlier in my pregnancy that I was expecting a girl, Mike and I had never quite believed it, convinced we would have another boy. I wished so much that my husband could be with me to share the moment, as I looked down at our first daughter. She had a spattering of dark hair, and when she opened her mouth, inside was a little front tooth. She was advanced for her years right from the start.

After I had cuddled and inspected her, Sarah was taken away to be cleaned up and I finally closed my eyes, exhausted. When I opened them again she was sleeping in a cot next to the bed and Mike was standing at my bedside looking from me to his new daughter with pride. Coming up behind him, the nurse said softly, 'You can hold her if you like,' and he gently lifted our daughter out of her cot and cradled her to his chest. 'Hello, princess,' he said. Even when we finally named Sarah after two weeks of deliberation, it was this nickname that stuck throughout her life.

Our home might have been cramped, messy and noisy, but Sarah loved it there right from the start. She hated going out. If we took her for a walk in her pram she made her displeasure loudly known, by whingeing until we were home again. She was a real family girl, at her happiest in her parents' arms, and in the end I got a papoose in which I carried her everywhere. Strapped to my chest, she would gurgle contentedly while I washed up, cooked or made the beds. Even at night, Sarah wanted to be near me. Like all babies, she would wake at unsociable hours demanding to be fed. With Mike still working nights, I would simply scoop Sarah out of her cot, lay her beside me in the bed and feed her. She could never settle back in her cot afterwards, so I gave up trying.

When Mike came home early in the morning he would find both of us curled up together, fast asleep, Sarah wrapped in her security blanket, which had previously been my sister Fiona's shawl. Fiona had donated it to Sarah on a cold winter's night when she was just three weeks old and from then on it went everywhere with her. As a toddler, she would sit and rub her cheek with it while sucking her thumb. She loved the smell of it when it was dirty, and used to frequently offer it to us, saying, 'Smell that.' At the time we thought it smelt awful, and I used to beg her to let me wash it. On the infrequent occasions that I managed to persuade her, she hated it, and it was off the line before it was even dry.

When Sarah was six months old, Mike's parents, Terry and Les, made us an offer we couldn't refuse. They were managing an off-licence in Sussex where accommodation was included, meaning that their house in Walton was standing empty, so they asked if we would like to live there. We thought it would be for a matter of months, but we ended up staying for three years. It was the biggest place I had ever lived in, with its three bedrooms and huge back garden for the children to play in. The family spent hours in that garden and some of my fondest memories are of that time.

It was there that Sarah, who had by this time turned blonde, started first to shuffle around on her bottom, wearing out her long frilly dresses, and later to walk. She spent most of her time toddling up and down the garden path, pushing a little pram we had bought her. I had suggested putting one of her dolls in it, but she wouldn't hear of it. She preferred to load it up with slugs that she had found in the flower beds, and she would walk the pram and its slimy contents to the garage at the bottom of the garden, where Mike and Terry tinkered with classic cars. Sarah would totter unsteadily over to Mike, asking 'What you doing, Daddy?', and he would scoop her up in his arms, and plant a big kiss on her small cheek, making her giggle in delight.

Being close together in age meant that the children were more like friends than siblings and always enjoyed playing with one another. Mike bought a swing set for the garden and the boys would strap Sarah into it and take turns pushing her. We told them to be careful and push her gently, as she was a fragile little girl and it didn't take much to start her crying. But the boys were always careful with her, naturally protective of their little sister, and enjoyed looking after her and teaching her things. Luke, who was fascinated by dinosaurs, spent hours explaining to Sarah the differences between the tyrannosaurus and diplodocus, using models. As the eldest, Lee was the first to have a bike with stabilisers, which he would perch Sarah on, and walk her down the garden path.

Behind the garage were trees and bushes, which Sarah was convinced housed fairies, elves and pixies. She would excitedly take my hand and lead me to the bottom of the garden, saying, 'Let's go on a fairy hunt!' Sarah loved anything magical. She firmly believed that there were all sorts of things in the world that you couldn't see but were none the less very real. God was one of them. Although Mike and I are not religious, from the very first day that Sarah was taken to a church with her class at school she was a believer. Later in her childhood, she and Luke – a firm atheist – would have long discussions about Darwinism and the existence of God that gave the rest of us pause for thought.

As many of Sarah's games involved make-believe and magic she had less use for toys than other children, but she still had her fair share of teddies and dolls. Her favourite doll was called Goldie, who had been passed in childhood from my sister to me, then to Sarah. Goldie was made of plastic, had movable arms, short yellow curly hair and a variety of clothes to be dressed in. Sarah also liked Polly Pockets, miniature dolls in houses or castles, like modern-day dolls' houses. Equally, she could entertain herself for hours with two sticks or pens that she made into people.

When Sarah was two I became pregnant with Charlotte and I explained to Sarah that she was going to have a sister, who would come out of my tummy. As a believer in all sorts of inexplicable things, Sarah didn't seem to be surprised by the idea. As my bump grew bigger, she would lie with her head on it, shrieking with pleasure when her unborn sister gave a kick. Mike and I worried that she would be jealous when Charlotte was actually born, as Sarah had been the centre of everyone's world all her life, but Sarah plainly adored her new sister from the start, despite their obvious differences.

Charlotte asserted her independence right from day one, and was more than capable of taking on the world. The night she was born she stayed awake for hours, her eyes wide open, looking around her. She simply didn't need the constant reassurances and cuddles that Sarah craved. But despite her sister's apparent indifference to receiving love, Sarah wanted to hold and care for her constantly. When we put Charlotte into her door swing, Sarah would spend hours bouncing her up and down. In fact, she became so obsessed by her that we eventually got her a new doll and pram, so she could have her own baby to cuddle.

When Charlotte was a baby I started taking the girls to the mothers and babies group at the local church hall. There was also a nursery there, and although initially Sarah was quite shy and reluctant for me to leave her, she gradually started to attend two mornings a week. By this time she had an invisible friend called Goggy and I suggested that perhaps he – or she, we never knew – should go with her. Taking a pal with her, even if they were invisible, boosted Sarah's confidence and she quickly settled down. There were three Sarahs in the group, so she started to call herself by her full name. When asked to introduce herself she would proudly say: 'I'm Sarah Payne.' Within no time she had quickly established herself as leader of the group, bossing the other children around. Yet despite her confidence, she was always incredibly fair-minded and sensitive to others. If a child was upset or their feelings hurt, she would be the first to try and make things right.

Despite her popularity at nursery, Sarah remained very family oriented and always preferred to play with me and Mike or her siblings than friends of her own age. She was constantly telling the family how much she loved us. She would bound up to me, throw her arms around my waist, and say, 'I love you, Mummy.' I always said, 'I love you too,' which usually prompted the question, 'How much do you love me?' I would then stretch out my arms as far as they would go and say, 'I love you this much', to which she would reply, 'Well, I love you this much', stretching her arms out as far as they would go. We often repeated this ritual ten or twenty times a day. Before bed she would always make sure she kissed everybody goodnight and she loved 'Eskimo' kisses, rubbing noses with each of us in turn. She was also a great one for hugs, and when Sarah put her arms around you there was so much feeling put into it that you really knew you were being hugged.

Yet despite all her lovely qualities, Sarah was no angel. Like all small children, she could be a right pain in the neck. She was very strong willed and could throw the most tremendous temper tantrums. Food was a big issue and dinner times were often a battle as I tried to get her to eat balanced meals. She hated vegetables and foods that were mixed together, like casseroles or spaghetti bolognese, which the rest of the family loved. Her favourites were fish fingers or chicken nuggets and chips with tomato ketchup, and they always had to be kept separate on her plate. She also had a really sweet tooth and would have eaten puddings every night if she'd been allowed to. When she came shopping with me – an activity she found she liked – she would shriek, 'Shop till you drop!' and demand sweets. When I refused her, or tried to get her to eat healthier food, she would get stroppy. Sometimes, when she didn't get her own way, she would explode, shouting, 'I hate you!' But as soon as the words were out of her mouth she would instantly regret it and two seconds later she would be apologising. After a row she never bore a grudge. Even when it was the other person who was in the wrong, Sarah would look at them with her big brown eyes, and offer a cuddle to make up.

When Sarah was four, the time finally came for Terry and Les to sell their house in Walton. While living above the off-licence they had taken their time looking for the perfect house in East Preston, and they had finally found it. It was set on a private estate called Kingston Gorse, surrounded by beautiful country-side and fields, the beach just minutes away. After they moved in we started taking the children down to visit at the weekends and in the summer, and they would while away many an hour playing in the garden, making sandcastles on the beach, or chasing one another around the fields. It was a children's paradise. As we never went abroad – partly because I was petrified of flying and partly because we didn't have enough money – those weekends were like holidays to us. The Isle of Sheppey, where my mum lived for a time, was also a favourite family destination, and between both sets of grandparents we hardly needed to go anywhere else.

Obviously the downside of Terry and Les having found a new house was that we had to move. By this time Mike was working as a paint sprayer at a factory – still doing nights – and I worked part time at our local pub, the Old House at Home. Yet even with both of us earning, with four children money was always tight and there was no way we could afford our own home, so the council found us a house on Arch Road in Hersham. It was smaller than we had become used to, but it had three bedrooms and suited us just fine. Mike and I have never cared about material things or money. As long as we could get by, we were happy.

It was at Arch Road that we really settled into family life. Now in our mid-twenties, Mike and I were more relaxed and confident parents than we had been when the boys were born. We spent many a happy evening at Arch Road with the children, being silly, giggling, singing, dancing, playing games, watching television and eating take-aways. We couldn't understand parents who wanted to farm their kids off to boarding schools or on to nannies, as we loved our children's company and wanted to be with them as much as we could. I wasn't much of a housekeeper and the place was always a mess, with toys strewn about the place and dirty dishes in the sink, but we all made a joke of it and when things got really bad we pulled together and blitzed the house. That was just the way we were: untidy, always late, and a bit haphazard about everything we did. We didn't see any harm in that. The important thing was that we were a very loving and close family who adored one another.

Soon there was an addition to our family – a pet kitten called Ziggy who had been bought to replace Danny, a huge gentle greyhound that had been the children's pet in Walton. He could knock Sarah flying with a swish of his tail – and frequently did – but she doted on him. When we moved to Arch Road Danny was plainly too big for the house and he couldn't seem to settle, so Mike and I sorted out a new home for him. The children were heartbroken and Sarah sobbed so much when his new owners came to take him away that we promised her a new pet to replace Danny. So we found Ziggy. He used to sleep in the girls' room, with its pink walls and black treble wardrobe for all their clothes and toys, tucked up with Sarah in her little single bed, both wrapped snugly in her security blanket.

Soon after the move Sarah started at Burhill school in Hersham. Sadly, her first year there wasn't as happy as it should have been, due to the worsening of an inherited hearing problem called glue ear. As a little girl she had always been slightly deaf, which meant that she often shouted rather than talked. It also affected her singing voice, which was atrocious as she was completely tone deaf, but it didn't deter her from belting out school hymns or pop songs at the top of her voice. Music was one of her favourite pastimes, and she loved nothing more than turning the stereo up full blast and dancing around the room to Steps and SClub7. Often Mike and I would join in with her, spinning her around, having our own little disco in the front room.

Sarah's glue ear had never really caused her any discomfort up until she started school, when she began to get ear infections regularly. She hated being poorly and there were many tears during that time as she lay on a bed I had made her on the sofa in front of the television. Finally the pain got so bad that something had to be done and the doctor suggested that she have grommets put in to stop the build-up of wax. On the day of the operation I took her to the hospital, where she was put in a little blue gown. Sarah was so scared of being put to sleep, but as soon as the pre-med drugs hit her system, she started to giggle, laughing at the ceiling, as if she were drunk. Fiona and I laughed with her, and the mood was lightened for a few minutes. I walked with her as she was wheeled into theatre, and held her hand as the doctors injected her with the anaesthetic. It was an awful moment. One minute she was giggling insanely and ten seconds later she was out cold. When she came round from the anaesthetic she was weepy and scared, but after a cuddle and some love she was soon back to her old self.

After the operation Sarah's ear infections stopped, her hearing got better, and she settled down at school. She was a bit behind in her classes from all the time off, but she tried hard to catch up and soon she couldn't wait to get to school in the mornings. A notoriously late riser, Sarah was now always the first member of the family awake. When Mike came home from his night shift at 7 a.m. Sarah would be up and about already, pottering happily around the kitchen. By the time I got out of bed she would have made her sandwiches – usually peanut butter and jam – and packed them in her pink heart-shaped Barbie lunchbox. Her friends had already progressed to modern square lunchboxes with cartoon characters on them, but Sarah loyally stuck with Barbie. After Mike went to bed I would walk the children to school every morning, as I had never learned to drive. The boys thought themselves too grown up to hold my hand, but Sarah always held tight until the very last minute, when she would give me a big kiss and a fierce hug goodbye.

At school the children developed talents in different areas. Luke had a scientific mind, Lee was into technology and electronics, and Sarah emerged as the artistic one. She loved to draw and paint, and her pictures invariably contained at least one family member – along with a fairy. Rainbows also featured heavily, as they were one of her favourite things. Whenever she spotted a multi-coloured arch in the sky she would chase it down the road, even if it were pouring with rain. At the end of the school day she would proudly present her pictures to me and I would stick them on the fridge or wall. Every year my mum would encourage Sarah's creative side by making up what she called an art box for the children. Through the year she would buy glitter, glue, crayons, pencils, stickers and felt-tips and present them to the excited children who would open it, saying, 'What's in Nanny's box this year?' The answer was always: 'Everything.'

Sarah also loved books, and before she learned to read herself she pestered us to read to her every night. Books with magical elements, like fairy tales and Enid Blyton's adventure stories, were always her favourites. Similarly, on video, she would watch *Sleeping Beauty* over and over again, entranced by the beautiful princess who was awakened from her long sleep by a kiss from a handsome prince. Another favourite was *Fairy Tale: A True Story*, about two girls, Frances and Elsie, who photographed fairies in their garden in 1917. One birthday Sarah asked for a magic wand, which she thought she might be able to use to conjure up fairies herself. She played with her wand so much that Charlotte got jealous and tried to get rid of it, by flushing it down the loo. When that failed she tried to snap it in half, and finally microwaved it! That was the end of the wand. Sarah had every right to be angry, but she took her loss with good grace and accepted the apology Mike and I insisted that Charlotte offer.

As she progressed at Burhill, Sarah started to get interested in hair and make-up. Although one side of her hair was always thicker than the other, she loved her golden locks which she spent hours putting up in different styles. The two sisters also liked playing with my hair, sitting on the bed brushing and plaiting it, or putting it in a ponytail. One Christmas we got Sarah a heart-shaped pink make-up set, complete with mirror, brushes, powders and lipsticks. She loved to make herself and Charlotte up, experimenting with all the different colours, before starting on me. If she went to a friend's house or party she would take a little bag with her make-up set in it and paint their faces for them, always the mummy of the group.

She could never understand why I didn't like wearing make-up, and I could never quite understand where she got her girliness from. Even when her friends climbed trees and wore jeans and trainers she refused to give in to peer pressure and stubbornly stuck to her frilly dresses. Mike and I have such big families that there were always clothes from cousins going spare and her aunties used to bring her round bagfuls to go through. She was never more excited than when she was assessing a new collection and would spend hours at a time trying them on, then coming downstairs to show them off and canvas our opinion. Sometimes she changed outfits six or seven times a day, and when Charlotte was a bit older the two sisters would put on fashion shows for us, after raiding my wardrobe.

Although she continued to spend a lot of time playing with her sister and brothers, as she got older Sarah started to form strong friendships at school. Her best pal was a girl called Sammy, a tomboy with long curly ginger hair. In some ways the girls were quite similar – both headstrong and wilful – but Sammy was more of a dare-devil than Sarah, who would always try to be a good girl and please her teachers.

In her last year of primary school Sarah's sense of responsibility led her to be chosen as a 'befriender'. It was a new scheme where the school chose a handful of pupils each year to be the eyes and ears of the playground monitors and to provide comfort for the younger children. The school bought a special bench where children could go and sit if they were feeling sad or had nobody to play with. It was the befriender's job to keep an eye on the bench and go and talk to or play with any children on it. Sarah, who always seemed wiser than her years and had a very strong sense of fair play, took the responsibility very seriously. When a child's feelings had been hurt in some way, she always knew just what to say to make them feel better.

It was a testament to how much she loved school that, at the end of term, Sarah would always cry her eyes out. But as soon as she was home she got into the holiday spirit. Occasions have always been marked extravagantly in our family and, after Sarah learned to write, there was a constant stream of cards and letters to mark every one of them. The autumn was everybody's favourite time of year, as there was something to celebrate every few weeks. We had Luke's birthday in September, Sarah's birthday and Halloween in October, bonfire night and Charlotte's and Mike's birthdays in November, and Christmas in December. Christmas was the most exciting occasion of all for Sarah because Father Christmas brought that touch of magic to it. At the beginning of the month, Santa – actually Mike's brother – would call the children 'from Lapland' and Sarah would excitedly tell him that she had been good all year and put in her present requests. As the boys got older they realised that Father Christmas wasn't real, but they never let on as they didn't want to burst Sarah's bubble.

Like Father Christmas, Sarah firmly believed in the tooth fairy, and would excitedly place lost baby teeth under her pillow at night. In the morning her eyes would light up when she felt under her pillow and found the tooth gone, replaced by a shiny fifty-pence piece. Once Mike and I forgot to retrieve a tooth and Sarah was dismayed to find it still there when she awoke. The next day she found a note from the tooth fairy under her pillow with a new coin. It said that she had been at a fairy ball the night before and apologised for not picking up the tooth. Sarah never suspected for a second that Mike and I could have left the note, and proudly kept it.

Halloween was another big occasion and Sarah would spend weeks thinking about what costume to wear to go trick or treating. On the Halloween just after she had started at Bell Farm – 'big school' – Sarah's plans were disrupted by a nasty accident. She was in her bedroom on the first floor when she heard fireworks outside. Opening the window, she leaned out in an attempt to see the colours in the sky. In her enthusiasm she leaned too far and fell right out. In the kitchen below, Mike and I heard a thud on the concrete outside, followed by a cry from Sarah. We were almost too scared to go out and look, but of course we did. By some miracle she had not broken any bones. She seemed to have bounced off the concrete and escaped with bad bruising which hindered her movement. She was sobbing her little heart out when we found her – from pain, shock, and the fear that she wouldn't be able to go trick or treating. I ended up taking her in a pram so she didn't miss out.

By bonfire night, a week later, Sarah was fully recovered. Eager to make up for a sub-standard Halloween, she was staying late at school to watch the fireworks display with her friends. She had been looking forward to it all week. At 8 p.m. Mike and I pulled up at the school gates to collect her, and she clambered into the car, her face half hidden by her school scarf and hat.

'Did you have fun tonight?' I asked, expecting a barrage of excited chatter about sparklers, Catherine-wheels and loud bangs.

She was silent for a long moment, then I heard a sob escape her, and she pulled her scarf up over her eyes. 'Oh my goodness, what's the matter, what's happened?' I asked, anticipating that she had fallen out with one of her friends.

For a long time she couldn't answer, as she continued to cry. Finally she managed, 'I'm sad about all the children who will get burnt by fireworks tonight and end up in hospital.'

That was typical of Sarah's tender nature, which shone through again and again, never failing to amaze me. On one occasion Sarah sat on the sofa crying her eyes out as she watched starving Bosnian children on the news. When the school encouraged the children to make food and toy parcels for the Bosnian boys and girls, Sarah boxed up every last one of her toys to send. Mike and

I spent hours persuading her that she should keep a few back for herself. She was so loving and soft that sometimes it almost broke my heart.

Sarah used to say that she wanted to be a teacher when she grew up and have a fairy-tale wedding with a dress like a princess. But looking back now, I realise that I could never picture her as an adult – I never saw my daughter with a future. From the moment she was born I simply learned to enjoy Sarah day by day. I don't know why this was. I'm not pretending it was a premonition or anything mysterious. Perhaps it was simply that Sarah was my third child and I had relaxed into motherhood, not fretting about the future, but enjoying the children for the moment. I simply loved being Sarah's mum.

2

ABDUCTION

Saturday, 1 July 2000, dawned a gloriously sunny day and it
seemed a shame to spend it cooped up indoors. Unfortunately I
had my usual lunchtime shift at the pub and Mike needed to get
some sleep after his night shift, but we decided to make the most
of the weather after that. The children were keen to go to the
seaside, so we thought we'd visit Terry and Les on the Sussex
coast, planning to go as soon as I finished work at 2 p.m.
Leaving the boys and Mike at home with instructions to tidy up
and prepare overnight bags, I took Sarah and Charlotte to the
pub with me, as I often did. There they spent a happy few hours
helping me bottle up before we opened, playing with Claire, the
daughter of the landlady, Angela, in the pub's massive garden,
and eating chips for lunch with the regulars.

The pub was busy that day so it was an hour later than
planned that Sarah, Charlotte and I finally left for home, eager
to get going to the seaside. When we walked through the door
Mike was emerging from the bedroom in his dressing gown,
looking bleary eyed. It immediately put my back up.

'Why aren't you dressed yet?' I asked him crossly.

'Sorry, I overslept, forgot to set the alarm clock,' he mumbled.

'Well hurry up, we're late enough as it is.'

I looked around – there were dirty plates in the kitchen sink, overflowing ashtrays on the window sills, toys littering the floor. It looked even worse than when we'd left. Oblivious to the mess, Lee and Luke were sitting on the floor in front of the television playing on the PlayStation.

'What have you two been doing all day?' I asked them, exasperated.

Lee shrugged, 'I dried the laundry.'

Walking into the kitchen I opened the drier, and pulled out the clothes – they were soaking wet.

'Lee!' I shouted, getting more annoyed by the minute.

'What?' he answered, his voice muffled from the computer.

'You set the drier to cold, nothing's dry.'

'Oops, sorry, Mum.'

None of us had anything else clean to wear, so I corrected the setting and put the clothes back in. Rallying the family, I gave out instructions to pack, wash and tidy while we waited for the clothes to dry. Mike was still half asleep and the kids grumbled at having to help, so we spent a tense hour getting ourselves and the house in order. Eventually I pulled on my clean jeans, which still clung damply to my legs, and shoved the rest of the clothes in a bag. We were ready to go at last.

It was 4.30 when we bundled the kids into our seven-seater Renault Savanna, and the ride down to Sussex was a quiet one. I was still annoyed with Mike for having slept in, and the kids were sulking because we had snapped at them. Charlotte slept most of the way down, Lee listened to his Walkman, Luke stared out of the window, and Sarah started on her new book, *Don't Be Silly, Mr Twiddle!*, by Enid Blyton. We had barely exchanged ten words between us by the time we arrived in East Preston just over an hour later. But as we pulled into Terry and Les's driveway the mood seemed to lift. Between the beautiful countryside and beach, it was hard not to feel happy at their house. As we got out of the car Sarah tugged at my sleeve. 'Mummy, look, I read a whole chapter all by myself,' she said proudly. 'Well done, princess, that's great,' I told her.

Apologising to Terry and Les for being late, we piled into the house, to smells of shepherd's pie cooking in the oven. There were hugs and kisses all round, drinks were poured, and we sat down at the table, beginning to relax. With her dislike of mixed foods, Sarah could be fussy about shepherd's pie, but that night – eager to please us all – she drowned it with tomato ketchup and cleared her plate. After we ate, Les, who kept a very tidy house, insisted on cleaning up, while Terry, Mike and I let our dinners go down and finished a bottle of wine. The children, fidgety from the car ride, were eager to go outside to play in the garden.

Not long after they'd gone, Les spotted a note on the desk. It was from Sarah, although I still don't know when she'd had the chance to write it. Les smiled as she read aloud, 'To Mrs Payne, I love you so so so so so so so much, Love from Sarah.' In case we hadn't got the message, Sarah ran back inside the house a minute later and launched herself into my arms, giving me one of her fierce hugs. She then repeated the same routine with Mike, Terry and Les, before rushing back out. It was typical of Sarah: she hated any bad feeling and this was her way of making up for the cross words we had exchanged earlier in the day.

After we had sat and caught up on everyone's news, Mike, Terry and I decided to go for a walk. A friend of Terry's had been doing up a house locally and he wanted to show us how nice it looked. Les, tired from the cooking and cleaning, said she would stay behind to relax in front of the television for a bit, while the children decided to come with us, as our walk took us along the beach, where they liked to play. The stroll down to the water only took five minutes and as soon as the kids saw the sea they took off, chasing one another along the shore, shouting and laughing. I could tell that Luke was itching to do his usual trick of diving straight in the water with all his clothes on, but he didn't quite dare with us watching him.

The plan was to carry on along the beach to Terry's friend's house, but Lee, Luke, Sarah, and Charlotte were enjoying themselves so much that they begged us to let them stay. 'Do we have to come?' Lee asked, 'Can't we stay and play here?'

It wasn't unusual for us to let Lee and Luke play by themselves on the beach when we were visiting Terry and Les, but we had never left the girls before. They were allowed to play in Les's and Terry's garden and driveway by themselves, and once or twice they had played in the field behind the house, but never further than that.

'I'm not sure Sarah and Charlotte should stay,' I told him, turning to ask Mike's opinion.

'Your sisters are still a bit too young,' Mike agreed.

'Don't worry, me and Luke will look after them, they'll be fine,' Lee pressed.

Every parent faces these questions at some point: at what age should you let your children play out by themselves? And what places are appropriate to leave them? At the age of eight Sarah had recently started to walk to school without me accompanying her. She walked with her friends, with Luke behind, keeping an eye on her. We mulled the current situation over: there were four of them, it was still light, and the beach was almost deserted. We couldn't see what harm they could possibly come to.

Then Sarah and Charlotte joined in, 'Please let us stay, we'll be fine.'

So we came to a decision: 'OK, you can stay, but Lee's in charge, so you have to do whatever he tells you, and be good.'

The girls smiled. 'Thank you!' said Sarah, and I leaned over to give her a kiss, before doing the same with Charlotte.

I then turned to the boys: 'If you get bored, go back to Nanny's house, make sure you're back before dark, and stay together.'

With that, we started walking away from them, back up towards the village. Sensing I was anxious, Mike squeezed my hand reassuringly and I turned and waved to the children, who were now splashing in the rock pools and collecting shells. Sarah, dressed in her blue Fred Perry tennis dress, her blonde hair blowing around her face, smiling and laughing, waved back.

We walked back up to the village where we admired Terry's friend's house, before stopping at the local pub for a quick drink. We didn't stay long as I was still slightly worried about the children, and by 7.45 we had started on our way home, stopping at the off-licence for some wine and beers for later. Armed with our bottles, we walked back through the fields behind Terry's and Les's house, where we saw, from a distance, Les standing outside, Charlotte clutching her hand, Luke and Lee wide-eyed, looking around them fretfully. I knew immediately that something was wrong.

Before we had even reached them, Les called out anxiously, 'Have you got Sarah?'

'No, of course not,' I replied.

'Well, she's gone,' said Les with desperation.

'What do you mean "gone"?' I echoed stupidly.

'Gone. She's disappeared. We can't find her anywhere.'

She had uttered the words that every parent dreads, and they threw me into an instant panic. I frantically looked around me, scanning the area for my daughter. Being the height of summer, the fields surrounding the house were overgrown with tall crops and bordered by unruly hedges. Streams crossed the land and, further down, beaches gave way to the sea. In a split second I registered with dismay that the wild landscape afforded endless places for a child to get into trouble.

I didn't stop to ask what had happened; there was only one thing on my mind – I had to find Sarah now. Snapping into action, I reached for Charlotte and pulled her with me towards the lane that runs along beside the house. Shouting 'Sarah, Sarah' at the tops of our voices, we frantically searched up and down Peak Lane, pulling aside brambles with our bare arms and looking under hedges. Meanwhile, Mike grabbed the boys and headed into the cornfield where they began beating back the crops, some of which were over four feet tall, to see if she was hidden there. Terry and Les disappeared back into the house to make sure their grand-daughter had not hidden herself away under the bed or in a cupboard, playing a game.

Within a few minutes we had reached the end of the lane. There was no sign of Sarah. Scooping Charlotte up in my arms, I jogged back to the house. Knowing Sarah to be a cautious type of child, I simply could not believe that she had gone far from home. I was convinced that she must be nearby and kept expecting her to rush out from somewhere, shouting 'Mummy, Daddy', and catapult herself into our arms.

As the family searched, the air punctuated by shouts of 'Sarah', the story emerged in bits and pieces. After we had left them, the children had become bored playing on the beach and decided to wander back towards the house to play in what they called the 'potato field', as their grandparents used to grow potatoes there.

In the field they started playing hide and seek and Sarah, being the fragile girl she was, fell over and hurt herself. Feeling out of sorts, she decided she wanted to go back to the house to see her nanny. The children usually used a gate in the field to get home, but for some reason the farmer had padlocked it that day, so Sarah started running towards the lane. Conscious of not leaving his sister alone, Luke started to run after Sarah, but just as he had nearly caught her Charlotte stung herself on a nettle. Luke turned back to tend to his younger sister, and Lee took over the chase for Sarah. When he was three-quarters of the way across the field, he briefly looked back at Luke and Charlotte, and when he turned round again Sarah was gone.

Lee ran back to the house where Les was watching the Lottery and knocked on the window. When she opened the door to him he pushed past her and searched every room, convinced that Sarah must be playing a joke on him. Eventually he told his nanny, 'I've lost her.'

Now I watched as he desperately swiped at crops and shouted his sister's name. Seeing Lee in a panic, when he was normally so calm, rattled me. My mind went into a spin: Sarah wasn't the type of child to run off or hide. If it had been Luke missing, I wouldn't have worried, as he was always wandering off, but Sarah got frightened on her own. Even when she played hide and seek, if she were left undiscovered in a wardrobe for more than two minutes she would emerge, looking scared. Maybe she had somehow got lost on her way back to the house. Or she might have had an accident and be lying injured somewhere.

We had soon searched the entire area around the house twice over and there was still no sign of her. Clutching at straws now, Les and I decided to go into the village in case she had wandered over there. The neighbours were having a barbecue that night and their guests' cars had blocked the driveway. We knocked on the door, explained to them what had happened, and they broke up their party to move the cars and help us search for Sarah. When the drive was clear, Les and I jumped in the car and headed into the village. There I stopped every person I saw, desperately repeating over and over again, 'Have you seen my daughter? She's eight with blonde hair, about this big', holding my hand vaguely in the air. People were concerned and eager to help, but nobody had seen her.

At one point we came across a group of children. My heart lurched as I saw that one of them was the spitting image of Sarah. When we asked them if they had seen her, they asked what she looked like. 'Just like you,' said Les, adding, 'If you see her, take her home to your mummy and call the police.' Soon it felt like we had asked everyone in the village and I was suddenly acutely aware that the skies would soon be black, and all I could think of was how Sarah was scared of the dark.

We drove back to the house, stopping on the way to speak to Mike and Terry, who were still out searching. We agreed that it was time to call the police, and once in the house I went straight to the phone and dialled 999.

Taking a deep breath I told the operator, 'I've lost my eight-year-old daughter. She's been missing about an hour and three-quarters now.'

'Right. Was she playing with anyone at all?' they asked.

By this point I wasn't thinking very straight. 'She was playing with her brothers and her little sister and she sort of walked away from them. They've gone to find her, she obviously took off though. The trouble is she is on holiday here.'

The operator asked for the address, then asked me, 'What's the name of the little 'un that's missing?'

'Sarah,' I said, a lump in my throat.

Telling the police that Sarah was missing made it all the more real and the panic inside me rose to a different level. The best way I can describe the sensation is like an air bubble growing inside you, rising up your throat. Your insides feel they are expanding until they might burst right out of you, and your heart beats so hard and fast you can almost hear it. But I knew I had to fight the unfamiliar feelings and stay calm and keep focused. Sarah was out there somewhere and our job was to find her.

The police arrived within ten minutes and soon the house and fields were bustling with activity. Helicopters equipped with infra-red searchlights were flying overheard within half an hour; hastily assembled search teams scoured the nearby fields and countryside; uniformed officers searched every house on the estate; and detectives went over what had happened with us, while turning Terry and Les's home upside down. They were searching in places that seemed silly to us – in kitchen cupboards, wardrobes and lofts. When we questioned them, they told us, 'You'd be amazed at the places kids turn up.'

The police paid particular attention to the children's stories, especially Lee's, as he had been the last person to see her. They kept gently stressing to him that any small detail could be vital. Lee had already been through his story once before he remembered that he had seen a white van in Peak Lane just after Sarah vanished. At the time he had no reason to attach any significance to it, but amazingly he remembered the van driver clearly. He described a white, scruffy-looking man with discoloured, gappy teeth. 'He smiled and waved at me,' Lee told the police. In retrospect, this turned out to be the single most important piece of information we received that night, but at the time we didn't realise it.

At 1 a.m. when the search was finally called off, to begin again at first light, I wearily took the children upstairs. When we stayed at Terry and Les's, all four of them slept in the same room, Lee and Luke in single beds, with Charlotte and Sarah in between on the floor, cuddled up together in a nest of blankets. The boys climbed into their beds wordlessly, exhausted from the night's events, while Charlotte pulled the covers over her on the floor. She looked very small and alone without Sarah beside her. Looking at me seriously, she asked, 'Where's Sarah, Mummy? When's she coming back?'

'We don't know where she is, darling, she's lost, but we're doing everything we can to find her,' I said, stroking her head, as I always did before she went to sleep. Sarah loved being stroked too, and my heart lurched as I realised I had one less child to touch that night.

Neither Mike and I, nor Terry and Les, got a wink of sleep that night. For the first few hours we sat together in the lounge, smoking like mad, drinking, going over the evening's events endlessly, wondering where Sarah could be. Then, as the night wore on, we fell silent for the most part, exhausted by the emotion. We were in a state of shock, wandering around the house or sitting staring into space like zombies, all lost in our own worlds. It almost felt as if this wasn't happening to us, like it was some sort of surreal out-of-body experience and that we were looking in on our lives, not living them. One by one, the family settled down in the lounge on sofas or armchairs and closed their eyes. Nobody was sleeping, but having your eyes shut meant that nobody would disturb you. As the temperature dropped, a cool draught blew through the room, but I wouldn't let anybody shut the front door. When Sarah came home I didn't want her to see a closed door and think we hadn't been worried about her.

As I lay on the sofa with my eyes shut, my imagination went into overdrive. I pictured Sarah falling in a ditch and breaking her leg, or tripping over the roots of a tree and knocking herself out. I could hear her in my head, calling for Mike and me, in terrible pain, unable to move, alone. People ask me now if I thought that she had been snatched, but I honestly didn't. The idea that someone might want to do her harm didn't occur to me at first. Of course, I had read about such things happening to children, but Terry and Les lived on a private estate with security in a sleepy village. The thought of a predator there who would kidnap a child was too outrageous to even consider. I could only think that some natural accident had befallen her and she was hurt.

Just before first light broke and the house was quiet, I sneaked outside to clear my head. Heading for the field where Sarah had been playing only hours before, I squeezed through a gap in the hedge. Stinging nettles brushed my arms, but I barely noticed. I walked from one end of the field to the other, calling my daughter's name. With just silence for an answer, I became increasingly desperate. Falling to my knees in the crops, which were slightly wet from the morning dew, I finally broke down and cried, great heart-wrenching sobs racking my body. With each heave of my body and each guttural cry, the panic and despair rose, threatening to overwhelm me. I was consumed by a terrible feeling of powerlessness. As a mum I was meant to protect my children and to know what to do if things went wrong. I had failed on both counts and I wasn't sure that I could stand it. If Sarah wasn't there, I didn't want to be either.

I don't know how long I stayed in that field, screaming and sobbing. I don't remember how I got back to the house – I think that a police officer found me there, took me back, and made me a cup of tea. What I do know is that when I had calmed down I made a conscious decision. I could not afford to give in to my emotions again or I would fall apart. And then what use would I be to Sarah when she came back? I was still convinced that it wasn't a question of *if* – it was *when*. I thought she would be scared, shaken and hurt, but I was still convinced my baby was coming home and I had to be strong for her.

First thing on Sunday morning we were introduced to family liaison officers Dave Dowell and Sean Scott. They were to be the point of contact between the police investigation and the family, keeping us informed of what was being done to find Sarah. We liked them straight away and over the next days, weeks and months they became almost like part of the family.

Soon after their arrival the search parties started to congregate in the field behind the house. We watched in amazement as over 150 police officers assembled, their numbers matched by members of the public who had heard about Sarah's disappearance on the news. The search co-ordinators took charge, and within no time lines of people had formed across the fields, on their hands and knees, slowly and methodically moving forward, searching for any trace of my daughter. Mike and the boys were itching to go out and join them, but Sean gently suggested that it might be better for us to stay in the house. He said it was to keep the family in one place, but privately I thought it was because they feared what they might find.

It was a hot day so we opened up the back of the Savanna in the driveway, as police activity bustled around us. As the search teams combed the countryside, helicopters circled overhead and an RAF Meteor flew over the village using infra-red equipment. Later that morning a police sniffer dog was taken into the cornfield to pick up any scent of Sarah. Our hopes were briefly raised and then dashed, when the dog appeared to pick up a scent after twenty minutes of circling the field, before bounding back towards the house. Seeing all the people, uniforms and high-tech equipment around us, in a setting that was usually so peaceful and tranquil, was surreal. It was almost like being on a film set – with the family in the middle, looking on, bewildered and helpless.

As the day wore on, family and friends arrived, pale and concerned, to offer their support. They joined us as we talked, wondering for the hundredth time what had happened to Sarah, smoking packets and packets of cigarettes. Sarah hated us smoking and we had tried to give up for her, but on that day we thought she would forgive us the bad habit.

As the afternoon turned into evening our anxiety built. The search teams had been out for twelve hours now and they had found no trace of Sarah. If she had got lost or had an accident, surely they would have found her by now? As the temperature dropped, we moved inside and sat around the front room, with Les making sandwiches that nobody wanted. For the first time we tentatively discussed the possibility that someone had taken her. Yet we still tried to think positively. We thought that she could have been snatched by a 'mother abductor' – that is, by someone who wanted to love her, not hurt her. There are women out there who can't have children and want them so desperately they would do anything to get them. And Sarah was so sweet, what person wouldn't want her as their own daughter?

Another possibility that went through our minds was that she had been kidnapped for money. Kingston Gorse is quite well to do, and anyone seeing a child playing there might assume that they came from a rich family who could afford to pay a large ransom for them. Both of these scenarios were terrible, but at least they left open the possibility that Sarah was alive and being looked after.

As the long day drew to a close, Mike put his arm round me and suggested we go upstairs and get some sleep, but I shrugged him off. 'You go,' I said, dismissively, and he trudged upstairs alone. I couldn't go to bed, I had to be downstairs in case Sarah came back. I may have dozed off for a short time, but for the most part I simply lay on the sofa driving myself mad with worry. Early in the morning, as I sat having my first cigarette of the day, there was a knock at the open door, and Dave walked in.

'Is there any news?' I asked straight away.

Dave shook his head. 'I'm afraid not. I came to ask you and Mike if you'd consider doing a press conference to appeal to the public for information.'

I didn't have to think twice about it: we would do anything to help find our little girl. The more people that knew she was missing, and could keep an eye out for her, the better. When Mike surfaced I told him the plan and he paused before slowly nodding his agreement.

Later that day we were taken to Littlehampton police station and introduced to Detective Superintendent Alan Ladley, the senior investigating officer, and Detective Inspector Martyn Underhill, known to everyone as Tosh because of his similarities to the character in *The Bill*. Before the briefing began, Martyn sat us down in a private room and told us that he had some news. Holding hands, Mike and I waited anxiously.

'We arrested someone last night,' Martyn began.

I don't know what I had been expecting, but it wasn't that. 'Who?' I asked immediately.

'A man who was in the area at the time Sarah went missing.'

Mike jumped in, his face a mask of rage. 'What's his name?'

'I'm afraid we can't tell you that at the moment. He's still in custody and we're questioning him. We'll let you know as soon as we have anything else.'

'Just promise me one thing,' I asked. 'Whatever happens, be straight with us.'

'We'll never lie to you,' Martyn said, 'but there will be certain things we have to keep to ourselves for operational reasons.'

I nodded my understanding, before Martyn talked us through the format of the upcoming press conference. He explained that we needed to make an appeal for information, but left the exact wording up to us. With that, we were led into the briefing room and sat behind a table in front of scores of television cameras, photographers and reporters. Beside me, Mike was literally shaking from head to toe, but I barely registered our audience. Alan introduced us and, staring at the cameras, I began to speak.

'You can't imagine what Sarah means to us,' I started. 'We're a strong family and we don't survive well apart. We need her home now, today, as quickly as we possibly can.' Taking a deep breath I continued, 'Her brothers and sister are really not coping very well without her. She's our life.

'Our family name for Sarah is our little princess, and that's just what she is. She's just a soft, gentle little girl. She hasn't got a horrible bone in her body.'

I ended with a direct appeal to the public. 'Somebody out there must have seen her. Maybe you don't think you did. But if you saw a little girl on her own that day, ring the police. Try very hard.'

When we got home I switched on the television, and there we were. I hadn't realised how terrible I looked until then. None of us had been near a bathroom to wash since Sarah had gone and the supplies in our overnight bags were running short. I had come to Sussex wearing a tie-dyed T-shirt and jeans. Unusually for me, I had packed some dressier three-quarter-length beige trousers and matching top, in case we went out somewhere nice. By the time the press conference came round, I was barely capable of dressing myself, let alone picking an outfit that matched, and I slung on the beige trousers with the tie-dyed T-shirt. There were dark black circles under my eyes, my long hair hung lifelessly around my face, and I wore no make-up. But appearances didn't matter. All that mattered was finding Sarah.

The next day we had a visit from Martyn and Dave, accompanied by a man we had seen on television but not yet met – Assistant Chief Constable Nigel Yeo. Les made us all some tea, and we sat around the kitchen table.

'You know we told you that we arrested someone on Sunday,' Martyn began. 'Well, we have some more information that you should know, before you hear it in the press.'

'What is it?' I asked, my heart pounding.

'The man is a convicted sex offender – a paedophile – who has previously abducted a child.'

While I reached for my cigarettes and Mike looked on with a face like thunder, Terry jumped in, 'Was it a boy or a girl he abducted?'

'A girl.'

'How old?' Terry asked.

'Nine.'

At this news, Mike got up and stormed out of the room and we all heard a door slam. I didn't have the energy to go after him.

Then Les asked the question we had all been thinking. 'What happened to her?'

'He assaulted her and then let her go,' answered Martyn. 'We don't know for certain yet if he had anything to do with Sarah's disappearance, but if he did, then there is hope that he hasn't harmed her.'

My head began to spin, as I considered for the first time that my little girl had been snatched by a paedophile. Yet the more I thought about it, the more ridiculous it seemed. I genuinely thought that nobody could bring themselves to hurt such a soft, tender-hearted little girl. I was convinced that if she had been snatched she would have won her abductor over within the hour. Sarah wouldn't have kicked and cried, like Charlotte would have, she would have been quiet and obedient, doing anything they asked of her. Even the most evil person in the world couldn't harm a child like that. There must be another explanation.

The beginning of the week passed by in a blur of activity. We started every day with a press conference, determined to keep Sarah's name and face in the public eye. For the most part we found the press very respectful, but there was one incident that really upset us during that time. We were taking questions from reporters when a girl from a news agency stood up. 'I spoke to Lavinia Tildesley earlier,' she started. 'Her seven-year-old son Mark was raped and murdered by a paedophile. She just wanted to say that she's thinking of you on this day.'

I couldn't believe what I was hearing. I looked at Martyn, who nodded at me, and we stood up in unison. 'This press conference is over,' Martyn told the assembled reporters and photographers. As I walked out from behind the table, I went up to the woman and said, 'You are a sad individual. My daughter's alive,' before making for the door. As I stood and waited for Mike, I heard Martyn saying to her, 'What the hell do you think you're playing at? You're banned from all further press conferences.' As he walked away, she burst into tears, but I felt no sympathy for her.

Martyn led us into an interview room and I promptly started to cry myself, saying, 'What a bitch, I can't believe she said that.' Martyn tried to calm me down. 'Don't listen to people like her. We're going to find Sarah.' I nodded, pulling myself together. He was right, we were going to find Sarah.

After the morning press conferences, there were always a hundred things to do. Lee and Luke were taken back to the cornfield by police to retrace their steps before Sarah went missing, capturing everything on video. A televised reconstruction was staged for *Crimewatch* to see if it might jog somebody's memory; in fact, it prompted more than 800 calls to the police. The search teams combing the countryside were continually finding children's clothes in the surrounding fields and every new object they found had to be carefully bagged and presented to us to see if it was Sarah's. None of the items ever were.

The children asked to visit the police incident room, and we took them to meet the team of officers who were working day and night, giving up their holidays and spare time to find Sarah. Lee was interested in the HOLMES computer system and the officers kindly let him type his details in, distracting his mind for a short time. Before the children left they gave the officers pictures they had drawn for them, and they hung them on the walls to spur them on.

There were also various sightings of 'Sarah' across the country during those days. At first, when a new one was reported, we were filled with hope. One sighting, at Knutsford Services on the M6, looked particularly promising. We listened intently as the police told us how a woman had come forward and said that she had seen a little girl crying in the service station ladies' toilets the day after Sarah went missing. Trying to comfort her, the woman asked her name. 'Sarah,' the girl replied. At this my heart sank – I knew for sure then that it wasn't my Sarah. Ever since her days at nursery, where there were three Sarahs, she had always introduced herself as 'Sarah Payne'. CCTV footage of the girl being led away by a man later confirmed my instincts, and I have often wondered since who that little girl was and why she was so upset.

The activity during the daytime was a blessing in many ways as it kept our minds occupied. In contrast, those first few nights were painfully long. We sat around the lounge, tired from the day's events, a drink in our hands, surrounded by family snapshots. Everywhere I looked there were images of the four children, playing in the garden or on the beach, or smiling shyly in school photographs. During those drawn-out nights I would gaze at the pictures of Sarah and talk to her as if she were in the room with us. I would plead with her to send us some sign to let us know where she was and whether she was safe. I would end by telling her, 'We're coming for you, princess.'

At 1 or 2 a.m. Mike and Terry would go to bed, and Les and I would sometimes hear them crying themselves to sleep as we sat up discussing where Sarah could be. After Les went upstairs I would often stay up, writing in a red diary. At 4 or 5 a.m. when the house was quiet, questions, thoughts and ideas would pop into my mind. Having nobody to sound them off, I would jot them down. It might have been an idea for the next day's press conference, or an area to search. Or I might put down a personal comment for one of the officers. Once the police took the children on a helicopter ride. Being scared of flying myself, I noted jokingly in my diary the night before the trip, 'What the hell do you think you're doing taking my kids up in a helicopter?!'

If I went to bed at all it would be approaching dawn before my head hit the pillow. I had moved my favourite photo of Sarah into the bedroom where Mike and I slept, positioned on the window sill by the bed. It was one of my favourite pictures of Sarah, then aged five. In the photo she is smiling cheekily at the camera, her long blonde hair swept loosely around her face by the wind. It was the last thing I saw before I closed my eyes and the first thing I saw when I opened them. On going to bed I would whisper goodnight to my daughter and on waking, after a couple of hours' snatched sleep, I would wish her a good morning.

As the days passed we were overwhelmed by the response from the public. Every morning we were greeted by Dave or Sean bearing sackfuls of post. There were letters, cards, poems and pictures from mums, dads, children, old ladies, schools and churches. Tony and Cherie Blair wrote, as did John Major and the Duchess of York, all offering their support. In those long days we read every single letter that came through the door, doing half-hour stints at a time, as we found it a very emotional experience. At first we tried writing back to people, but we quickly found that it was too hard.

A surprising amount of the post we received was from, or about, victims of abuse, often children. One letter that sticks in my mind was from a pastor at a school who told how one of her pupils who was being abused by her uncle found the courage to come forward after watching us on television. On the whole, everyone was careful to be positive and refer to Sarah in the present tense, elderly people being the exception. One woman in her eighties told us how she had been abused as a child and it had ruined her life. She said that wherever Sarah was, if she had been interfered with, then she was better off dead. It sounded harsh but she meant well.

One of the most precious things I received during those agonising days was a gift from a woman in Loughborough. I unwrapped the package carefully, revealing a chain of sparkly clear beads similar to a rosary. Attached to it was a delicate fairy, with a gold body and crystal wings. My heart leapt at the poignancy of it as, of course, Sarah adored fairies. With the fairy was a card with the words, 'Come into the enchanted garden, it's the most magical place to be, and when three o'clock arrives, it's time for fairy tea'. I put the jewellery around my neck, and was rarely seen without it in the coming days.

Amazingly, not all of the letters wished us well – although we didn't get to see these at the time. The police intercepted all the post to the house and would take it away and open it, in case there was anything that might upset us. I remember just one letter slipping through – a tirade of abuse aimed at the family, accusing Terry and Mike of having killed Sarah. It hit Mike hard.

'What kind of sick bastard could write this?' he shouted.

'Ignore it,' I told him. 'They don't know you or Sarah, or the relationship you have.'

Ripping the letter into pieces he ranted, 'Do people out there really think I could harm a hair on my daughter's head?'

I put my hand on his shoulder. 'People don't think that. It's just one stupid, spiteful person.'

But of course it was something that the police had to consider – that one of the family had something to do with Sarah's disappearance. Martyn had told us from day one that while none of us were suspects as such, we all had to be eliminated from the inquiry. Luckily, this didn't prove too difficult, as there were receipts from the off-licence and eye-witnesses from the pub who placed us all together at the time Sarah went missing.

As the first half of the week turned into the last, and there was still no sign of Sarah, the likelihood that she had been snatched by a paedophile grew increasingly likely. It wasn't something the family talked about openly among ourselves – we couldn't bear to – but it was a scenario the police had prepared us for. A week after Sarah's disappearance, Martyn came to the house and sat us all down.

'We have to ask you something very important,' he said, 'and I want you all to think very carefully before you answer.'

We all nodded.

'Do you know anybody called Roy Whiting, or does the name mean anything to you?'

I didn't have to think carefully as I had never heard the name before, and I shook my head, as did Mike.

'Terry, Les?' Martyn prompted. 'What about you?'

Terry asked, 'Is this the man you arrested?'

'Yes, it is. We have to determine whether he was known to the family, whether he might have spoken to or seen Sarah before.'

'I don't know the name,' said Terry.

'Nor me,' said Les.

Seeing that we were upset by the conversation, Martyn reminded us of a case the previous year, in January 1999, where two little girls had been kidnapped in Hastings. Against all expectations, they were found alive several days later in their abductor's flat. We took this example and clung on to it as a ray of hope.

In my heart I was convinced that Sarah was still alive and when the police suggested making an appeal directly to her abductor, I quickly agreed. Although Mike would have done anything to help find his little princess, he was more reluctant, as appearing in front of the cameras turned him into a bag of nerves. He suggested I do the press conference on my own, but I felt I needed him there holding my hand, even if he said nothing. Finally, we agreed that I would do the talking.

Sitting in front of the television cameras I begged, 'Please bring my baby back. She is our baby - bring her back. Just bring her home. Drop her off at the end of the road or put her somewhere where she can be found. Don't be scared or frightened - we are not concerned with you. Just drop her off and let her walk away from you.'

I then spoke to Sarah. 'If you are watching now, we are coming to find you as soon as we can, darling. We will be there.'

I had promised myself that first night that I would not be dragged down by my emotions, and I stuck to this religiously. I refused to let thoughts of Sarah being abused or killed even enter my mind. I just wouldn't let myself go there, almost physically forcing the thoughts out of my head. I was absolutely determined that I should stay positive and, strange as it sounds, I remained certain that she was alive and that we would get her home.

My belief that Sarah was alive was reinforced when Sean and Dave asked us to prepare a 'go-bag', a hold-all that contained everything Sarah would need when she was found. They told us that the clothes she was wearing would have to be taken away immediately for forensic examination, so we should buy her new ones. Les and I went into Littlehampton where we choose a pair of pink pyjamas, a pretty nightie, a bright-orange loose-fitting summer dress, a pair of trousers, some slip-on shoes and underwear. We lovingly folded them into the bag and added *Mr Twiddle*, the book she had been reading before she disappeared.

Last into the bag was one of Sarah's most treasured possessions – her teddy bear, Wally, named after the old man who used to live next door to Terry and Les. Wally, who had since passed away, had always given the children sweets when they stayed with their grandparents. When Sarah complained one day that he had got the wrong flavour, I was embarrassed by her rudeness, but Wally kindly went and bought her an old-fashioned Paddington bear instead. The bear was from a local jumble sale and had obviously been well loved through his life, but Sarah loved him even more. We knew that Sarah would want to see Wally when we found her.

It was during the preparation of the bag that we had one of our only disagreements with Sean and Dave. They told us that if Sarah had been abducted and was found alive, that only I could go to her. Mike would have to wait in the wings. They reasoned that if she had been taken by a man – the most likely scenario – the last thing she would want would be men around her. Mike was furious.

'She's my little girl too,' he shouted. 'How will she feel if I'm not there for her when she needs me most?'

I agreed with him. If Sarah had been hurt she would need her dad to make it better. It was a point we would not concede and eventually the police gave way.

As the second week stretched on, exhaustion kicked in. I had been living on adrenaline since Sarah went missing and I was now reeling with tiredness. Rather than staying awake all night I started going to bed and falling into a coma-like state of unconsciousness. Curled up on my side of the bed, I had no dreams, there was just a big blank until I woke again the next morning. Sometimes Mike would try to cuddle me, but I couldn't accept the physical comfort he was offering. It was all part of keeping myself strong and in control of my emotions. If I had abandoned myself to my husband's arms and felt his tears on my face, I would have broken down.

There was no right or wrong way to deal with the situation, and the family all differed greatly in their emotional responses. Les and I were determined to keep busy and positive, all the time planning for Sarah's return. Somehow we thought that if we didn't think of her as gone, then she wouldn't be. The men of the house were more emotional – and realistic. Terry would regularly collapse in tears, great sobs that seemed all the more poignant coming from a big man who was usually so composed. Les later told me that he had said to her in those early days, 'She's not coming back, you know.' Les replied, practical as ever, 'Let's not think like that now, we'll face it if we have to.' She was his rock over that time, supporting him, while dealing privately with her own emotions.

Mike was, in turn, angry, silent, and mad with grief. The thought that somebody could have hurt his little princess was more than he could bear. During those days Mike and I barely communicated emotionally, being so wrapped up in our own feelings. He would take himself off for long periods of time, in the garden or at the neighbours'. Once alone he would sob quietly to himself, holding Sarah's purple beaded bracelet that he had carried in his pocket since she disappeared. At other times he would scream and shout. One day we were driving home after an outing to the village and he leaned his head out of the window and screamed at the top of his voice, 'Sarah, where are you?'

During this time, I'm sad to say that Lee, Luke and Charlotte didn't get the attention from us that they needed. Dealing with our own grief was so consuming that we sometimes forgot that the children needed help in dealing with theirs. One day, early in that second week, I was given a painful reminder of how badly this was affecting them. It was early morning and I had walked into Peak Lane, looking for some time to myself. In the distance I spotted Luke. His back was to me, and he was kicking and hitting out at a tree, flailing at it with his arms and legs, making noises of pure frustration and anger. My instinct was to run over and put my arms around him, to contain his anger and soothe him, but I stopped myself, realising that it was his only form of release.

Unlike Luke, who had always been the demonstrative one, Lee held his anger and grief close to his chest. Since Sarah's disappearance Lee had had to shoulder an enormous amount of guilt and responsibility for a boy of his years. As the one who chased after Sarah, he constantly berated himself for not having started after her sooner, or run faster. As if this wasn't enough, having seen the white van and its driver, he was the sole witness.

He was conscious that the breakthrough in the case could rest with him. To make matters worse, as he would be a witness if and when the case came to court, we were not allowed to talk to him in any detail or question him about what had happened, for fear we might cloud or influence his recollection in some way. It was a terrible burden for a thirteen-year-old to carry, and he had almost visibly aged overnight.

Charlotte was needier than she had ever been, becoming very dependent on us. She could not bear to be alone for a minute and was rarely quiet, keeping up a constant stream of questions and 'Mummy, Mummy' or 'Daddy, Daddy'. It didn't help that she didn't have any of her own toys with her and we were too preoccupied to buy more. Sean and Dave often saved the day. They would take the children out for burgers and make Charlotte laugh by driving round the roundabout twenty times. Sean started bringing her toys and videos from his daughter. She watched *The Little Rascals* twice a day, bringing us some respite and her some happiness. Charlotte and Sean sang along with the songs from the video, 'You are so beautiful . . .', and she would momentarily forget that her sister and best friend was gone.

It was so hard to know what to tell Charlotte as we thought she was too young to understand why someone would want to abduct a child. So when she ran from room to room shouting 'Sarah, where are you?', as she had taken to doing, we told her, 'Sarah's not here, darling, she's lost.' But even at the tender age of five Charlotte had already pieced some of it together in her own mind. Sitting on the floor with a photo of her sister in her hand, tracing her finger around Sarah's face, she would look up at me and ask, 'Has somebody taken Sarah? When are they going to give her back?' It was hard to know what to say: we were all asking ourselves the same questions.

3

MURDER

Since Sarah's disappearance seventeen days earlier, we had made
sure that there was always somebody in the house, in case there
was any news. To stop us going stir crazy, cooped up in the house
all day, we had got into the routine of going out in shifts. On the
morning of Monday, 17 July, Mike and Terry had gone shopping
in nearby Rustington while Les and I stayed behind with the
children. We had been sitting in the garden in the sunshine for
around an hour, chatting and drinking tea, when there was a
knock at the door. I strolled through the kitchen and opened it,
revealing Sean, a serious expression on his face.

'All right, Sean?' I asked in a light tone.

'I have to speak to you and Mike on your own now, nobody
else,' he responded grimly.

I moved aside, letting him in, and walked through the front
room where the children were watching television, and into the
kitchen. Looking back I can see that the signs were bad, but by this
time I was such a believer in the power of positive thinking that I
could successfully block out most sinister thoughts. I thought if I

repeated the mantra, 'Sarah is alive and she is coming home' enough times – and really believed it – it would come true.

'Mike's not here,' I said. 'Cup of tea?'

'Sara, I really need to talk to you now,' said Sean urgently.

It was gradually filtering through to me that there was something very wrong, but I was in no rush to hear what.

Putting the kettle on, I said firmly, 'Not without Mike. I don't want to hear anything until he's here.'

I turned and strode outside, followed by Sean, and sat back down at the garden table with Les, arms folded.

'What's happened?' she asked.

'I don't know, I don't want to know without Mike here too. It's not fair.'

Sean sat with me. 'Please, Sara,' he implored.

But I was adamant.

Les took charge of the situation and stood up. 'I'll try the mobiles,' she said.

While she made the call I refused to meet Sean's eye, and we sat in silence as we listened to Les telling her husband that they needed to come home immediately. When she took her seat again at the table we sat for what seemed like hours – although it was only ten minutes at the most – not speaking, anxiously flicking our eyes towards the door. After a lifetime of waiting, Mike and Terry finally appeared.

In contrast to my stony look, Mike's eyes were already red and swollen. He had obviously spent the ride home crying. 'What's happened to Sarah?' he asked immediately, choking on his words.

Sean started, 'I think you and Sara should hear what I have to say alone.'

But I cut him off. 'Terry and Les can stay.'

Clutching Mike's hand, I looked at Sean and took a deep breath, gathering all the internal strength I had left.

Sean began, speaking in an official tone he had never used with us before.

'At just past 11 o'clock this morning we got a call. A little girl's body has been found in Pulborough.' He paused, then continued, 'We don't know yet if it's definitely Sarah, but as no other child that age has been reported missing, it looks like it is.'

From somewhere that seemed far away I heard Mike shout, 'NO, not Sarah,' and with those words I finally cracked. I felt that the rug had been completely pulled out from under my feet. I had been so sure, despite what everyone had tried to prepare me for, that Sarah was still alive and I would get her back. I had simply not allowed myself to think of her being gone for ever. Now the unthinkable had happened and seventeen days' worth of pent-up emotion finally came pouring out. I put my head in my hands and just wailed. Mike put his arms around me and we sobbed together, our tears mingling as they ran down our cheeks. Through my sobs I managed to say, 'I want to see my little princess.'

Then all mayhem broke loose. Lee, Luke and Charlotte rushed into the garden, looks of panic on their faces that were intensified when they saw the state of Mike and me.

'Is it true?' shouted Lee.

Now I knew why Sean had been so keen to tell us quickly – he didn't want the family to hear it on television. Now it was too late, there was no opportunity to sugar coat it. 'We don't know for sure,' I said, and staggered out of my seat to gather the children to me. But my legs wouldn't support me, and I collapsed to the floor. Lee and Charlotte fell with me and we sat there huddled together, crying. Meanwhile, Luke turned and ran full pelt back towards the house. I stumbled to my feet, and went in after him. The front door stood open and I ran outside into the lane. When I reached Luke he was crying and shaking, utterly broken by the news. I just held my son to me, his head against my chest, and together we sobbed our way back to the house.

When we got back, the family were in the driveway. I looked for Mike, but he was nowhere to be seen. 'Where's Mike?' I demanded.

'He's gone for a walk, he needed to be by himself for a bit, love,' said Les. 'Probably best to leave him.'

I nodded. I knew Mike well enough by now to realise when he needed time alone. All around me were tears and raised voices, everybody speaking at once, firing questions at Sean. We all needed to know what would happen next.

Sean explained. 'We need to formally identify the body to see if it's Sarah. We can do it forensically, through dental records and DNA, so there's no need for you to go through the trauma of seeing her.'

'I want to do it,' I said.

'I really wouldn't recommend that,' said Sean. 'The body we found has obviously been there for some time, so it's not in a good state. If it is Sarah you can always decide later if you want to see her.'

At that moment I didn't have the strength to argue, so I let it go.

Now there was nothing to do but wait. When everything calmed down we sat, in a stunned sort of silence, as we had done that first day Sarah went missing, in open cars in the driveway. For some reason nobody seemed to want to go back in the house. None of us doubted that it was Sarah, but while we did not know 100 per cent we were in an eerie sort of limbo, with a tiny glimmer of hope in our hearts. Later that day the news that we had prayed wouldn't come finally arrived. Sean appeared at the front of the house.

Without any preamble he said, 'It's Sarah, I'm so sorry.'

There were no more tears then, like earlier, just a numb sort of feeling. Even when faced with the final confirmation that my little girl was dead, I couldn't quite believe it or take it in.

'How did she die?' I asked.

'We won't know until the postmortem is done.'

'Can I see her now?'

'I really don't think it's a good idea, Sara,' replied Sean.

But I wouldn't give in. I was determined to see Sarah because I didn't think that I could accept that she was really dead until I witnessed it with my own two eyes. Yet Sean was equally determined that I shouldn't put myself through the horrific experience. Finally, we struck a deal.

'I'll go and see her myself,' said Sean, 'and I'll tell you exactly what she looks like. If you still want to go, then I won't stop you.'

I agreed, privately resolving that I would go whatever he told me.

That night we stayed up, a drink in our hands, going over and over what had happened. Even now, when our worst fears had been realised, we found it so difficult to accept that somebody had actually wanted to kill our soft little girl. So we looked for any explanation for her death apart from the true one.

I said to Mike, 'Maybe somebody hit her with their car, panicked and buried her body.'

'Or,' Mike suggested, 'if somebody did kidnap her, maybe they didn't mean to kill her. Maybe he suffocated her by mistake when she was crying.'

We even talked over the possibility that she had died from fright, as we didn't see how a fragile girl like her would have been able to handle the situation. Although we knew in our hearts that none of these scenarios quite fitted, they gave us some comfort that night.

After a few hours' sleep snatched in the early hours of the morning, arrangements were made for us to visit the field where

Sarah had been found. We thought that it would help make it more real for us. Pulborough was just fifteen miles away, but it seemed to take for ever that morning. When Mike, Terry and I finally pulled up alongside the field on the A29, there was an eerie quiet, as the police and press had been moved away to give us room to visit undisturbed. We got out of the car, supporting each other, clutching a bunch of pink lilies. Sarah's favourite colour was pink and she had always loved fragrant flowers, so they seemed the perfect choice.

Alongside the field rows and rows of bouquets, cuddly toys and messages from the public had been laid down and it really hit me then how much the public had taken Sarah to their hearts. We stopped, and I bent down to read some of the tributes. With a teddy bear there was a note that read, 'Goodnight, sweet Sarah', while a bunch of purple and cream flowers bore the message, 'God bless, little princess'. Seeing our special family name for Sarah made the tears spring to my eyes again and I gulped them back.

Slowly, we walked through the gate, into the field where Sarah had been found. The white tent that we had seen on the television news that shielded her body had been taken down out of respect for us, the place where she had lain now marked off with yellow police tape. As Mike, Terry and I walked towards the far end of the field, hanging on to each other's arms to stop us from falling, we were silent, lost in our own thoughts. Somehow I had expected the field to be a horrible place, because of what had happened there, but of course it wasn't. It was simply a patch of slightly overgrown grass bordered by hedges, like every other field for miles around.

As we walked towards the tape, what struck me the hardest was how far into the field she had been left. I could not help picturing somebody carrying her body there to hide their wickedness. They had had so little respect for my daughter and for us that they had dumped her body like a bag of rubbish and left it to rot. With one anonymous phone call they could have let someone know where she was, so we could say goodbye properly. But they even denied us that.

True to his word, Sean went to view Sarah's body that day. After our visit to Pulborough, he gathered me, Mike, Terry and Les in the lounge and described every detail of what he had seen. At first I wasn't listening to him properly. My mind was so set on seeing Sarah that I didn't think he could say anything to change my mind. I kept interrupting him, saying, 'Just take me to my daughter, I want to see my baby.' But he eventually made me listen, and as he described the overwhelming smell as you stepped in the morgue, I finally grew quiet. It was a smell like you had never smelt before, he said, a smell so awful you reeled and thought you would be sick. When you finally saw Sarah's body, it was no longer recognisable as a little girl. After so long outside in the elements, with the wild animals, her hair was gone, she had almost no face left, her fingers, hands and toes had been eaten by animals, and there was no white skin left on her body, only grey decaying mess. And all the time the smell surrounded you, making your eyes water.

As he finished his description, he said gently, 'I don't want that to be your last memory of Sarah, when you have so many good ones.'

Yet even after all he had told us, I still said desperately, 'But we'll see through all that. We'll still know it's Sarah.'

Looking into my eyes, Sean spoke directly to me. 'That was not the little girl I was hoping to meet, the little girl that you have described to me and who I've seen in pictures and videos. I'll never forget what I've seen today for the rest of my life.'

Mike, who was holding my hand tightly, said to me, 'We can't, we can't go, Sean's right, that can't be what we remember.'

So finally, although I didn't really want to agree, I felt I had to. I sighed and nodded my head. 'OK, we won't go. Sarah wouldn't want us to see her like that, it would almost kill her again.'

Although it may have been the right decision at the time, it left me with an awful nagging doubt in the back of my mind that is still there to this day: was it really Sarah? When I was thinking straight, I knew that it was, as the forensic tests had proved it without a shadow of a doubt. I had given the police Sarah's hairbrush and one of her baby teeth that she had left under her pillow for the tooth fairy, for comparison. But without seeing her with my own eyes I couldn't quite believe it, and I kept thinking back to cases where mistakes had been made. It's part of not wanting to let go, clinging on to any hope, no matter how small or how silly, that this terrible thing hadn't happened.

I kept those thoughts to myself for the most part, knowing they were irrational, but Charlotte voiced them for me, as children do. She kept saying, 'But how do we know it's *really* Sarah, Mummy, how do we know for definite?' I tried to explain to her that the police had done tests. I said that when we go to the doctors and to the dentist everything is written down, like Sarah's grommets operation and the injuries she'd got falling out of the window at Halloween. I told her that pictures had been taken of her bones then, and that these were compared to the little girl's body they had found. She nodded like she understood, but half an hour later she was asking again, 'But how do we know for *sure*?' It was a bit easier with the boys as Lee was older and Luke had always been interested in science, archaeology, dinosaurs and fossils, so he understood how DNA could identify somebody.

Trying to explain the concept of murder to the children was very hard. Children usually only experience the deaths of elderly people, like their grandparents, who have been ill. They can understand and accept that everybody dies when they get old, but the idea that a young person can be killed on purpose is almost too much to comprehend. We told Charlotte that a bad man had taken Sarah away from us, and she wasn't coming home. We said she had gone to heaven. When someone dies the instinct is to make it nice for children, but we didn't want to make heaven sound too nice. The situation was far from nice – it was murder. She kept asking us over and over, 'But why?' and we answered honestly, 'We don't know. Some people are just built that way, they want to hurt little children.'

Later that Tuesday night we were told that the first postmortem on Sarah's body had been completed. The results dashed any hope that her death had been a tragic accident: Sarah had been murdered. Gruesome as it sounds, we wanted to know everything that we could about our daughter's last moments: what had been done to her, how long it had taken, how much pain she would have been in. We had to know the truth because our imaginations were running wild. Yet the postmortem did not shed much light on the matter.

We were told that Sarah had been strangled or suffocated – the pathologist could not be more specific because of the advanced level of decomposition. She had obviously looked for evidence of sexual assault, and concluded that Sarah had not been raped, which we took some comfort in. We thought that it would have made the end quicker and less traumatic for her. Yet it could not be ruled out that she had been interfered with in other ways and the police told us that in cases of child murder, where the child is found naked, it is almost always a sexually motivated crime. One thing they told us did provide us with some relief, however. According to statistics on a database run by the Derbyshire constabulary, when a pre-pubescent girl is abducted and not found within five hours, then she is dead. This made it highly likely that Sarah had been killed the night she had been snatched and her agony not prolonged.

As I could not go and see my baby and say goodbye I wanted to send her something from the family. At the end of that terrible day, I stood in front of the mirror and looked at the fairy around my neck. Reaching round, I undid the clasp and pulled it free. It was the first time I had taken it off since it had been sent to me. Now I handed it to Sean and asked him to put it with Sarah in the mortuary. I wanted her to be buried with it. Next I walked into the bedroom and opened the wardrobe door. Inside was the 'go-bag' the police had asked us to prepare. It would never be needed now. I reached inside, took it out and, sitting on the bed, I unzipped it. On top of Sarah's new clothes lay Wally. I cradled the bear to my chest, and lay on the bed holding him for a minute. I would send Wally to be with Sarah too – but not just yet. I needed him now.

That week the extended family, who had rallied round while Sarah was missing, left us alone to let the news sink in. For the first few days we were like robots, just functioning to stay alive. None of us ate properly, although well-intentioned people would drop round casseroles and other dishes to tempt us. Although we could not eat, we hit the booze hard. In the morning we would sort out whatever practicalities we needed to, and at midday we would crack open cans of beer or bottles of wine. From that point on we would drink steadily all day and late into the night. We weren't drinking to get drunk, but to take the edge off the pain. It acted as a sort of anaesthetic and helped us cope.

Sitting in a drunken haze, we would torture ourselves with the 'what ifs', the alternative scenarios that could so easily have played out and spared us this pain. What if we had not gone down to the coast that day? It hadn't been a long-standing plan, and we could so easily not have gone. If only we had stayed in

Hersham, this wouldn't have happened. Then my mind flickered to the bad feeling there had been among the family when we left home that afternoon and my heart lurched. Or I would beat myself up with the thought that if we hadn't left the children alone on the beach Sarah would still be here. We had been sitting in the pub having a drink at about the time Sarah was taken. What kind of parents did this make us? There was so much guilt that it was almost too much to bear. What it came down to was this: if we had been a more conventional family, your average Mr and Mrs Jones, with clear sets of rules, would this still have happened to us?

At the beginning of that week our emotions were out of control, changing quickly and without warning. One minute we would be consumed by grief and sadness, sobbing until we thought our hearts would break. I only ever did this when I was alone, but Mike could break at any time, anywhere. These spells might be followed by a kind of numb disbelief and denial. After that wore off came the guilt, the blame, the obsession with the details. Then, for Mike, there was the intense anger and the constant struggle not to give into his dark thoughts. When he started down that path, thinking about what that monster had done to Sarah, he almost self-destructed. On those long nights he would sit describing in minute detail what he wanted to do to Sarah's killer. He talked about abducting him, like he had done Sarah, and torturing him until he begged for mercy. He said he would like to cut off parts of his body and watch him bleed and suffer. It upset me to hear him talk like that, but I knew it was a natural reaction. Yet it wasn't mine: for some reason I could not feel any anger towards Sarah's killer.

Since Sarah's body had been found on the Monday, we had received numerous requests for interviews, relayed to us by Chief Inspector Mike Alderson, the press liaison officer. For the first couple of days we were too distraught to even consider it, but we had to address it at some point.

'Let's leave it,' Mike said. 'While we were searching for Sarah we needed help from the press to find her, but now she's gone there's no reason for us to do any more.'

'But surely we owe them,' I argued. 'We used them to get our messages across before and the whole country became involved. It's unfair to cut everybody off now. They may not have known Sarah, but they shared in our grief and they deserve some sort of closure too.'

Mike Alderson tentatively offered his opinion. 'It's up to you, of course,' he said, 'but it would be helpful to us if you made a personal appeal for information to find Sarah's killer. If there are people out there who know something, they may be more likely to come forward if you appeal to them directly.'

I looked at Mike. 'I think we should do it.'

He reluctantly agreed, and a press conference was scheduled.

On Thursday morning I wrote down some points I wanted to make, but in the event I threw the paper away and spoke from the heart.

I began, 'First of all I want to thank everyone for your support and, thank God, we have found her now. The family is devastated. It hasn't sunk in yet. We have got a job now, and that is to catch this person or persons, or whoever it is.'

At that point my voice faltered and I wasn't sure if I could carry on. I was grateful when Mike, usually so silent in front of the cameras, jumped to my aid, saying, 'We don't want this to happen to anybody, ever.'

With his support, I regained my composure. 'We can do that by being here, by talking to police, by keeping all of us together and making people remember.'

I then appealed for help from anybody who had seen a white

van in the area that night, before Mike spoke again. 'They've watched us suffer, they've watched our family go through something it should not go through.'

I picked this up. 'They've torn our children apart and they could have done something about it by picking up the phone. We can't even see our daughter because it's too hard and it's not *Sarah*. I don't think anyone should be allowed to do that to anybody. We believe in justice, and death is too good for this person. So help us find him, her, them.'

Working as a team now, Mike took over. 'The whole thing was just senseless. I mean, to take a girl like that. For what reason would you do this to someone?'

I carried on. 'And watch us go through it? We'll find whoever did this. I feel no pity for you any more. It hasn't sunk in at all, it hasn't. We're still waiting for the police to come and say they've found her, even though Sarah is already found. It's so unfair.'

At the same time as coming to terms with our grief, there were practicalities to consider. The funeral was the one that loomed largest in our minds, yet we had no idea when it would be. The police had told us that it could take some time for Sarah's body to be released as they had to do so many tests on her. We knew that if they were to find her killer they needed to do things right, so we told them to take their time with her and do everything necessary. Yet although we knew this was the right thing to do, it left us in limbo, unable to say goodbye to our little princess. We felt that we couldn't move on to the next stage – whatever that might be – until we had done something to mark her passing.

Dave was the one to come up with the answer to our dilemma as we all sat round the table one day: a memorial service. The more we discussed the idea, the more we liked it. It would give the family a way to grieve while we waited to bury Sarah. It also had another function – we could make it an open invite and give something back to the public. The response had been so overwhelming during the time that Sarah was missing and after she was found, that I felt we owed them something, a way to say goodbye. As we wanted the funeral to be a private affair, for family and friends only, this was the perfect compromise.

Guildford Cathedral was an obvious choice for the venue, as it was halfway between Hersham and East Preston, and was big enough to hold hundreds of people. We picked Saturday, 12 August as the date, and the week before was busily spent planning the type of service we were going to have, giving us all something to distract ourselves with. The family were agreed that we didn't want it to be a mournful event, partly because there would be lots of children there, but instead a celebration of Sarah's life, so we asked people to wear colours rather than black. We also decided that we wanted people who had actually known Sarah to conduct the service, rather than a vicar who had never met her, so we asked family and friends to give readings. When they asked for guidance of what to say, we simply said: say whatever you feel, speak from the heart.

When the family arrived at Guildford Cathedral that sunny morning, we were amazed to be met by nearly a thousand people who had come to say goodbye to Sarah. Some of them were known to us, including friends, colleagues, police officers, Sarah's school mates and teachers, and people from our village. But there were also hundreds of people we had never met before: families, old women, couples, children, many clutching flowers or notes of condolence. It was hard to believe that so many people were there to say goodbye to my little girl.

Inside the cathedral me, Mike, the children, and our parents sat together at the front. Although the first three rows had been set aside for family, there were so many of us that some relations ended up sitting in the alcoves as the cathedral quickly filled up to capacity. Standing in front of us was Sarah's school photograph, captioned 'Little Princess'. A newspaper photographer had offered to enlarge it and it stood 6 feet by 4 feet, surrounded by flowers and teddies. As we were waiting for the service to begin I held Mike's hand on one side of me and hugged Charlotte closely on the other, stroking her hair. For once she was quiet, her eyes downcast, looking so grown up in her little blue summer dress. We had wanted the service to be upbeat, but as the sound of children crying echoed round the cathedral, I realised this was probably unrealistic.

The service began with Sarah's favourite hymn, 'All Things Bright and Beautiful', which the whole congregation rose to sing. After the cathedral was silent once more, Sarah's form tutor, Jonathan Good, was the first to speak. Sarah had always had special relationships with her teachers, and Jonathan was her favourite.

He began, 'Sarah has painted so many pictures in our minds through her cheerful and enthusiastic outlook on life.'

Jonathan then went on to give the little details that made up his recollections of Sarah: how she laughed with friends as they held handstand races in the playground, and brought little presents to school for teachers and classmates.

'She would skip up and hand over the little treasures such as a picture she had drawn, a story she had written, or a necklace she had made with such a cheerful and gleeful face. She was a happy little girl, always smiling and chirpy, full of determination, with a strong spirit, just like the rest of her family.'

At this last thought I gave Mike's hand a squeeze and he returned the pressure.

After we all sang 'Morning Has Broken', Sarah's Auntie Fiona stood up. The memorial service held its own special poignancy for her:

'Five years ago today Sarah followed me down the aisle as my bridesmaid. She looked beautiful in a flowery dress with a hoop underneath and a floppy hat.' Determined not to give in to her tears, she then told how Sarah would sit in the garden giggling as she taught her three-year-old cousin how to paint her nails with felt-tip pens.

She ended, 'Our little Sarah has gone from us, but she will live in our hearts for ever and will always be remembered as Sarah, our little princess.'

The next person to rise was my best friend Jenny, whose daughter Mazie was Charlotte's pal. With a slight tremble in her voice she said, 'I became increasingly aware that each memory is accompanied by the crystal-clear sound of Sarah's giggle. To me, her unerring sense of humour, her ability to make the gloomiest of faces light up with laughter and her total inability to curb the giggles even in mid-sulk were the very essence of Sarah's short life.'

She continued, 'So whilst we sit and cry a million tears for the beautiful little girl who painted rainbow colours into the lives of all who knew her, we should remember that to truly keep Sarah Payne's memory alive, we must never forget how to laugh.'

The best thing about the service for me was that it gave me time to simply sit and listen to people who actually knew my daughter speak about her in a real way. For weeks we had been hearing Sarah described by the media, who had never met her. Now at last we could hear from those who really knew and loved her. When Jenny talked about rainbow colours and giggles, she was remembering the child rather than the murder or the disappearance, not the girl on the front pages but the real living Sarah. All of the readings touched me and captured Sarah, her life and her spirit, the reality of her.

To end the service Sarah's Uncle Keith read out a poem he had written for her. He had been working on it all week, and it captured my daughter's most loving qualities perfectly:

> Her giggle,
> Her smile,
> Her adorable face.
> Her hug,
> Her kiss,
> Her loving embrace.
> Her warmth,
> Her charm,
> Her indomitable spark.
> Her energy,
> Her zest,
> Her indelible mark.
> Her sweetness,
> Her love,
> Her gentle ways.
> Her belief,
> Her trust,
> Her joy in our praise.
> Her faith,
> Her bond,
> With her sister and brothers.
> Her closeness,
> Her devotion,
> To her father and mother.
> Etched in our hearts,
> And undiminished,
> Remains forever,
> This endearing image.

After the service we filed out of the cathedral for a final act of remembrance. When we had first announced that we were having a memorial service, a firm called The White Dove Company called and offered us a basket of twelve white doves to release in memory of Sarah. We thought it was a lovely idea, just the sort of thing Sarah would have liked. As I walked outside I noticed Sammy, Sarah's best friend, with her mum, Diane. We had seen them the week before and Diane had told me that her daughter was utterly devastated by Sarah's death, unable to even sleep on her own any more. I had suggested that it might help to write her feelings down. Now she told me shyly, 'Mum got me a book and I write to Sarah when I miss her and feel unhappy.' I smiled at her and took her hand, saying to Diane, 'Can I borrow Sammy for a minute?' She followed me to where the white basket of doves was waiting. We all gathered round, and Mike lifted the lid off the basket and the doves struggled free. They rose into the air and hovered for a moment, before flying up into the sky and circling overhead. As they did, I imagined Sarah's spirit rising with them, soaring over the cathedral and away.

4

THE FUNERAL

We had prepared ourselves for a long wait to bury Sarah, but shortly after the memorial service we were given the unexpected news that her body would be released to us at the end of the month. It was a huge relief. Some parents whose children have been murdered have to wait months to bury them, and some don't get to do it at all as their little bodies lie undiscovered year after year. So in this way we felt lucky, as burying Sarah would enable us to say our goodbyes and take a step forward – both emotionally and physically.

During the time that Sarah was missing and afterwards, while her body lay in the mortuary in Sussex, we could not contemplate going back home to Surrey. We felt we had to be near her. But now that she was to be buried we knew the time was approaching to go home. We wanted Sarah's funeral to be in our local church, St Peter's in Hersham, where she had spent so many a happy hour. From a practical point of view, the timing also meant that the children would be back for the first day of school in early September.

Yet going home raised a whole new set of problems. After Sarah went missing we had tried, once, to go back to Arch Road, after Fiona had cleaned it up and discreetly packed away Sarah's things. But in the event we could not bring ourselves to go inside – the memories would have been too much – and we all agreed that there was no way we could ever live there again. Yet we could not get ourselves together to address the problem. Jenny saved the day. Without me knowing, she got in touch with the local council and asked them if they could move us, and they swiftly arranged another house. We didn't have to do anything except agree, which we gratefully did, site unseen. Fiona and Jenny packed up our house, thoughtfully putting all Sarah's things into plainly marked boxes so we wouldn't open them by mistake and get a shock. Jenny's husband Ian then loaded up his van, moved all the stuff to our new house, and it was done.

With this load off our minds, we spent our remaining time in Sussex planning our daughter's funeral. We decided on 31 August as the date, and asked Sarah's vicar, the Reverend Nick Whitehead, to conduct the service. Mike was adamant that Sarah should get the send-off she would want, which meant a lavish one. She had always loved marking occasions and she had been eagerly looking forward to mine and Mike's tenth wedding anniversary. She had begged us to renew our vows, so she could be a bridesmaid and see us before the altar, but she died before her wish could be granted. She had also spoken of getting married when she was a 'big girl', telling us she wanted a 'princess's dress'. As there would never be any fairy-tale wedding for her, we wanted to give her the most perfect funeral we could think of. It was the only thing left we could do for our little girl: bury her like the princess she was.

Leaving Terry and Les's house after two months was an

emotional upheaval for us in many ways. But when Sean and Dave came to pick us up to take us to our new home on the eve of Sarah's funeral, we knew it was the right thing to do. We hoped that it would mark the end of a chapter in our lives and be the start of happier times. Terry and Les came with us, to help us settle in, and we were grateful not to have to wave goodbye to their support just yet. As we pulled up outside our new end-of-terrace house in Riverside Road, with its garage and back garden, we should have been pleased, as it was much nicer and bigger than Arch Road. But as we trudged inside with our bags, we couldn't bring ourselves to care. Going upstairs I looked at the three bedrooms and quickly assigned them: Mike and I in the double, the boys in the next biggest, and Charlotte in the box room.

'This is your new room, Charlotte,' I said to her.

She looked crestfallen. 'But Lee's and Luke's is bigger. It's not fair.'

Charlotte and Sarah had always had a bigger room than the boys, as they had so many toys and clothes. But with Sarah gone and Charlotte in her own room for the first time, the boys needed the bigger room. Charlotte knew this, but it seemed too cruel to point it out again.

I stooped down. 'It'll look nice when you've put your posters up. Maybe we can get you a new Westlife one – or even David Bowie. What do you think?'

She still looked unsure. 'Maybe . . .'

I tried again. 'Why don't you sleep in the big room with your brothers tonight? You can play on the computer.'

'OK,' Charlotte agreed happily, and the small room was momentarily forgotten.

As the day of Sarah's funeral dawned, I awoke feeling eerily calm. I dressed in a black dress with a grey print on it and a

long black coat; applied some make-up, and put my hair up.
When I looked in the mirror I hardly recognised myself. People
started arriving at the house from early in the morning and we
all gathered in the back garden, where Mike poured everybody
a stiff whisky. Everyone there was family, with the exception of
Dave and Sean, whom we had asked to join the funeral
procession. They said they would be honoured. As we sipped
our drinks I fiddled with the wisps of hair around my face that
had broken free from the clip. I have always felt uncomfortable
when I tie my hair back and that day was no exception, so I
reached up and pulled the clip free, letting my hair tumble
down my back. When Mum looked at me questioningly I said,
'I really need to be myself today,' and she nodded her
understanding.

We waited for Sarah to arrive for what seemed like an age.
Finally, we heard the clip clop of horseshoes, and the family
moved to the front of the house where an ornamental black
carriage drawn by four grey horses pulled up. Inside was a little
white coffin, surrounded by floral tributes: purple and white
flowers that spelt 'Princess Sarah', a teddy bear wreath, and a
floral cross. It was beautiful, and Sarah would have loved it,
but as I stood there looking, all I could think was: 'Her coffin
is too tiny. It isn't right.' Sarah had always been so larger than
life that it simply didn't seem possible that she had been reduced
to this.

We had decided against funeral cars, opting instead to walk in
a procession behind Sarah to the church, which was only 500
yards away. Silently, the family began to form a line behind the
carriage. Mike and the boys led the way, with Terry pushing my
dad Brian in his wheelchair. Behind them walked me, Charlotte,
my mum, Les, and my sisters Maria and Fiona. The rest of the
family and Dave and Sean followed behind. The roads had been

closed off, shops and businesses were shut, and the streets were lined with villagers who had come to pay their respects. I walked slowly and silently, holding Charlotte's hand. Dressed in her blue-and-white polka dot dress, I'm not sure she understood exactly what was going on as she looked around her, bewildered. One minute she would be grimly looking at the ground, and the next she would break into a skip. She knew that it was Sarah in the carriage as we had been to see her coffin in the chapel of rest a few days before, yet she still had a lingering feeling of disbelief. At the chapel she had asked us over and over, 'How do we *know* it's Sarah, how can we be sure?' We patiently explained, but she ignored us. 'But someone could have taken her away and she could be somewhere else,' she protested, putting into words what we all wished so hard for.

As we arrived at St Peter's church, the carriage stopped and I watched as the doors were opened. Again I was confronted with how very small her coffin was as the pallbearers lifted it on to their shoulders with ease. We followed Sarah again, as she was carried carefully into the church, holding one another for support. St Peter's was already full to capacity, with some 300 mourners, including family, local schoolchildren, Mike's work colleagues, regulars from the Old House, and villagers. We had originally planned the funeral as a totally private affair, but after various media requests we agreed on a compromise: inside the church was family and friends only, and loudspeakers were put in the field outside which was full of the press.

After Sarah's coffin was placed by the altar and we were seated at the front of the church, my predominant feeling was one of total disbelief, similar to how I had felt on 1 July, and again on 17 July. I thought: 'This can't have happened, this is not real, it's not right.' I kept asking myself, 'Why?' Had Mike and I really been that bad in our lives that we deserved this? Had we been such irresponsible parents? We had always had a relaxed attitude with the children, but we hadn't allowed them out to play by themselves at all hours. In fact, Sarah had lost her life during one of her first snatches of freedom. It was so unfair. I felt physically and emotionally sick. The child inside me wanted to stamp my feet and say: 'I refuse to do this, I can't do this.' But then I looked at my other children and pulled myself together. I had to do this, I had no choice.

For a few moments the church was totally quiet, then, as the service began, I could hear people around me begin to cry, some softly and some more vocally. But my eyes remained dry, as I sat holding Mike's arm, which shook with the rest of him. I knew that I had to keep it together if I was going to get through my reading. I had been undecided at first whether to speak, unsure of what to say. Eventually I remembered my own advice to those who gave readings at the memorial service: speak from the heart. And so I decided to write to Sarah. When the time came, I stood and walked the few steps to the front of the church.

My hand trembled as I held the letter before me and started to speak, 'I didn't know what to write, so I just wrote to Sarah.' I paused to take a breath and began:

'Dear Sarah, ever since you came bounding into our lives at two in the morning, with no phone in the house, one tooth in your head and a smile that would melt ice, we loved you.

'You were the joy that made our lives full. In the house, under the garage with your pushchair full of slugs and woodlice, you talked to us for hours. Dad called you Princess – because that's what you are.

'You'd never rise before 10 a.m. and when you started school we thought you'd never get up. But you loved it. You loved your friends and you loved your teachers.

'When you had your grommets put in, you were scared. Then you were drunk on the pre-med and still giggled. Most of all, you were brave – but never quite brave enough to have your ears pierced, though we got to the shop several times.

'As a sister you were great. Lee misses your chats. Luke misses your rows. And Charlotte . . . she misses you. Your stories, your songs, your games, and most of all your huggles. As a daughter, my darling' – at this point I could not stop the tears – 'Oh, Princess, you were perfect. Love always and for ever, Mummy and Daddy.'

I sat down and wiped the tears away as the service ended and we filed out of the church. But as the song 'I'll Find My Way Home' by Vangelis sounded out over the loudspeakers, I couldn't hold it in any longer. Mike and I have always loved that song; it is so haunting that it gives you goosebumps, and we always said we wanted it for our own funerals. It seemed so appropriate for Sarah when she was missing: 'I'll Find My Way Home'. But she never had. There were crowds milling around us and Charlotte was clinging on to my leg, yet I was aware of nothing at that point but the song and Mike, who was literally holding me upright. My legs were buckling, but he held so tight and didn't let go. For those few moments, as the coffin was put back in the hearse, Mike and I really connected and for the first time in two months we felt like one again.

After the burial, which I remember almost nothing of, we went to the pub. We arrived in the afternoon and stayed until closing time, getting very, very drunk. It was so confusing – I didn't know how we were meant to act, whether we should be mourning Sarah's death or celebrating her life. That day I felt like we were the children, rather than the parents, in need of guidance and care. As the evening wore on, we fired up the juke box and danced with abandon to The Jam. Jenny and Ian, and our other friends and family, were all brilliant. They hugged us, and drank, and danced, going along with whatever we wanted, never questioning what we needed to do in order to get through.

The day after the funeral Mike made an announcement that took me by surprise. 'I'm going back to work on Monday,' he said.

'Don't you think it's a bit soon?' I asked. 'Are you sure you're ready?'

'I need to get back to some normality. If I hang around the house all day I'll dwell on things and go mad.'

I knew immediately where Mike was coming from. His manic depression could hit him at any time and put him out of action for weeks. Surprisingly, he had not lapsed into one of his episodes after Sarah's death, but we were both always acutely aware that it could happen at any moment. Going back to work might head it off.

Like Mike, the boys were keen to get back into a routine. When school started again they grabbed their lives back with a vengeance, catching up with their mates, riding their bikes, and playing football. They were as devastated by Sarah's death as the rest of us, but they needed to be normal boys again. Yet although I understood this, and wanted to encourage it, it was hard for me to give them their independence back. Since Sarah's death I had kept the children close to me at all times and now I had to face letting them go again. Unable to supervise them as I would have liked, I started imposing strict rules that they had never had before, insisting they came home immediately after school or, if I had agreed to let them go to a friend's for tea, they had a curfew of 8.30 p.m.

One night they arrived home to find me sobbing my heart out on the sofa. They were ten minutes later than promised and I was out of my mind with worry. I knew it was irrational but I couldn't help myself. The boys were very understanding and apologised for being late, but a few days later they sat me down for a chat, like they were the adults and I was the child, which in a way was true at that time.

'Look, Mum,' said Lee, 'we know how you feel about us being out on our own, but you've got to lighten up a bit. We'll do our best to always be on time and let you know exactly where we are, but sometimes we might get a bit held up and you can't collapse every time.'

I nodded. 'I know you're right, I'm sorry, I just can't help it.'

Luke piped up, 'We worry too, you know, but we would never put ourselves in any danger. And we're never really alone anyway, there's always a few of us, and we've always got our mobiles with us so you can call if you're worried.'

They were absolutely right. I had to back off and allow them to grow up. Being with their friends was good for them, it got them out of the oppressive atmosphere of the house and took their minds off what had happened. When they were with their mates they could be normal boys again, not the brothers of Sarah Payne, as they had become in the newspapers. I knew it would be hard, but I had to make an effort to let them be.

As the youngest, and a girl, Charlotte bore the brunt of my over-protectiveness. I took her to school in the mornings and brought her straight back home in the afternoons. After that time she was rarely out of my sight. If she wanted to play with friends they would come to our house, where they went to Charlotte's bedroom or played in the garden with me watching them. Sometimes at the weekends we went for walks in the woods. Previously, I would have let the children run off ahead, out of sight, but not out of hearing. Now I held Charlotte's hand tightly. Afterwards we might go to the Old House, so

Mike and I could have a drink. I knew it wasn't fair to keep Charlotte cooped up in the smoky pub, so I reluctantly let her play in the back garden, which was totally fenced off from the road. But even then I would get up and check on her every ten minutes. When she spotted me I would pretend to be collecting glasses to help out, but even at that age she could see right through me.

Since her sister had gone we had noticed, little by little, that Charlotte simply wasn't herself any more. Gone was the independent strong-willed madam we had come to expect, replaced by a helpless little girl. Just trying to get her dressed was an ongoing battle.

'Run upstairs and get dressed, sweetheart,' I would tell her.

'I can't,' she would whine, 'you do it, Mummy.'

'You know how,' I'd say, 'be a big girl.'

But she shook her head, looking so lost and sad that I would take her upstairs and help her on with her clothes. It was distressing to watch, as she had been dressing herself since the age of two, stroppily insisting, 'I can do it,' when we tried to give her a hand. When Sarah died, suddenly Charlotte couldn't do anything for herself any more. She had been at nursery school since she was just two and a half so she had always been advanced for her years and already loved books. Sarah had started reading to her younger sister in their bedroom at night before they went to sleep. They both loved Enid Blyton books, with *Mr Twiddle* and *The Magic Faraway Tree* being their favourites. But Charlotte, now six, hadn't shown any interest in books since Sarah had died. It was as if Sarah's death had retarded her development, wiping her mind clean.

Charlotte's room had become like a shrine to her sister. She became obsessed with the cuddly toys that the public had left for Sarah after her body was found. There were literally hundreds of every sort of animal you could imagine that the police had bagged up for us, and Charlotte's wardrobe was now full to bursting with them. She also kept every single one of the ribbons from the 30,000 bouquets of flowers that were left. For a long time she wouldn't let anyone else touch them. Eventually, when we thought the obsession was getting unhealthy, we persuaded her to donate some toys to a charity called Miracles, which was going out to Kosovo. We told her that she could choose one type of toy to keep, and she picked the Winnie the Pooh characters, including Tigger, Piglet and Eeyore. She then persuaded us to let her keep all the Beanie Babies as well. In all, eighteen bags went to Kosovo, while Charlotte kept five.

As the school term progressed, the family became increasingly weary. When we had moved back to Surrey we thought that life would return to normal, but we hadn't taken into account just how emotionally and physically drained we all were. Everything we did took a monumental effort. Simply getting up on time, making breakfast and walking to school seemed like huge challenges some days, and it was as much as I could do to get myself to the shops and make tea for the family. Just a couple of weeks into the new school year, the exhaustion finally caught up with us. Just as I was dragging myself out of bed, Lee walked into my bedroom, hair tousled, black circles under his eyes.

'Mum, I don't want to go in today.'

'Why not?' I asked.

'I just don't want to. I'm tired, and Luke's still asleep.'

'OK, go back to bed,' I said, getting back in myself and pulling the covers over my head.

If the children couldn't face going to school, for whatever reason, that was OK with me, I wasn't going to make them. They had been through enough, and life was too short. Charlotte was still asleep, so I left her, and when Mike came home he got into bed and none of us woke again until midday.

This set a pattern. Some days, when we could all face it, we got up together and went through the morning routine. But increasingly there were days when none of us even woke up until lunchtime. Charlotte almost never wanted to go to school, waking up exhausted after terror-filled nights of bad dreams. I would lie awake in bed next door, hoping night after night that the screams would not come. But they always did. She would dream of being trapped in the back of a white van or a bad man taking her away from us. When she woke crying and shouting, her bedclothes thrown off her, her pink silk Little Miss Naughty pyjamas twisted, I would always run to her. But when she was in that state she wouldn't let me touch her, holding her hands out, warning me to keep my distance. Respecting her wishes, I would sit on the bed, repeating, 'It's OK, it's OK, you're safe,' until she was calm enough for a cuddle. She had developed a terrible fear of being kidnapped, and refused to sleep anywhere near a window. One night she stayed at a friend's house and her mum ended up sleeping with Charlotte on the bathroom floor, in a little tent she'd made. It was the only place she felt safe.

When Charlotte asked to stay at home I was almost glad, in a selfish way, as it meant that I could keep her within my sights. We felt safer when we were together and didn't have to face the dangers of the world. Yet although my instinct was to stay in the house, it was there that I felt my worst, as a dark cloud had descended upon the place. People kept telling me to get out, but when I did try to leave the house it felt like disaster after disaster. Jenny would come round every morning to see me, and one day she said, 'Right, you need to get out, get your coat, we're going for a walk.' So we did. The first person we met along the road told me that my mum's best friend had died. Almost every person we saw after that stopped me and said how sorry they were about Sarah. They meant well, but I didn't need the constant reminders. We walked to the local shops and I got some dinner for later: frozen pizza and chips, and six chocolate desserts. It was not until I reached the till that I realised I had bought Sarah's favourite pizza – plain cheese and tomato – and had one extra dessert. Seeing my mistake brought reality flooding back. There was one of our family missing and there always would be. 'Can we go home?' I asked Jenny weakly, and she took my arm and led me away. When we got back home, my best friend turned to me, joking, 'Next time I tell you that you should get out more, don't take any notice of me.'

But Jenny didn't give up in her efforts to bring me out of myself. A few weeks into the school term, she and Ian suggested that the two families take a trip to Selsey on the coast, for a caravan holiday. At first Mike and I were reluctant. After all, our last weekend away had led to Sarah's death. But the children were keen to go, and we felt we owed it to them to try and be the parents they used to know, who liked being silly and having fun. Since 1 July, if one of us even cracked a smile, or laughed, we would instantly feel guilty for feeling any pleasure. We knew this was something that had to change, for the sake of the other children, if nothing else. So we agreed to go and try to have a good time.

On the first night we all went to the campsite club. There was a main room with a bar, tables and chairs, and a dance floor, and a back room for the children, where they held dance competitions and sang karaoke. We didn't like the thought of the children being out of our sight, even though the back room was supervised, so Jenny and Ian offered to be the sensible adults that night and not drink too much so they could keep an eye on them. With that worry off our minds, we drank heavily, even by our standards, downing pint after pint of lager. We had been drinking constantly since Sarah went missing, but it was not to get drunk, merely to numb us. But it brought us down, not up. That night, though, we got drunk like we used to: happily, stupidly, falling over, giggling drunk. I got up on the table and grabbed the mike off the DJ, singing along, off key, with whatever disco classic happened to be playing. The children ran happily between rooms and Mike danced with abandon on the dance floor, spinning Charlotte around and around as she squealed with delight. It was the closest we had come to being our old selves since Sarah's murder.

Yet towards the end of the evening, perhaps because of the drink, I felt my good mood start to be clouded by some paranoia. By now most of the country knew who we were and wherever we went we were recognised. That night was no exception and as I was singing and dancing I would occasionally catch somebody staring at me. When I returned their gaze they would quickly look away, but I could see in their faces that they recognised us. Nobody said anything or even looked disapproving - I think they actually thought, good for you - but I suppose deep down I had the sense that we shouldn't be behaving outrageously in the circumstances, that we should be staying at home crying and mourning for Sarah.

As the club closed at midnight we started to gather the two families together to go back to the caravan. Since Sarah's death it was a process we always found stressful. If one of the children was out of sight or earshot when we called them together, we immediately panicked. That night the children were quickly accounted for, but Mike was nowhere to be seen. I assumed he had gone to the gents, but after ten minutes of waiting around he still hadn't appeared. They were clearing the hall, so we went to wait outside. Mike was there, having a cigarette – he simply hadn't bothered to tell anyone. Before, it wouldn't have been a big deal, we would have shrugged it off, but after Sarah's murder everything got blown out of proportion. As we started the ten-minute walk back to the caravan we began bickering, all the good cheer of earlier in the evening suddenly gone.

'Why did you leave me there?' I asked him.

Mike replied, 'I didn't leave you. I just went outside for a fag.'

'Well, you should have said. I was worried.'

'Where did you think I'd gone?'

'I didn't know – that's the point,' I almost screamed.

'You're being ridiculous, Sara,' he shouted back.

Soon the argument had turned into a full-scale fight, and Jenny and Ian gathered the children and took them ahead back to the caravan. By the time we got back we were pushing, shoving and hitting each other. The fight was no longer about what had happened back at the club. It was about nothing – and everything. It was us venting our grief and frustration. Mike never needed an excuse to scream and shout, but for me it was only after a few drinks that I could really let down my guard. The rest of the time I was obsessed with keeping control of my feelings. As we continued to scream outside the caravan, Ian came out and tried to calm things down. But, stupid as the fight was, neither Mike nor I would back down. In the end I stomped into the caravan, leaving Mike outside. Always the peacemaker, Ian suggested that he and Mike go for a walk, and by the time they got back we had both calmed down.

As a family we usually thought of autumn as the beginning of the festive season, as there were so many occasions to celebrate, but without Sarah we just wished it would disappear. The toughest of all was Sarah's birthday on 13 October, when she would have been nine. That morning we took coloured lanterns to her grave, as Sarah had always hated the dark, and later in the day we released purple balloons with Sarah's name on them in a local park with her old school friends. The press were there to do stories, and although I had agreed to it, part of me resented their presence. I felt that Sarah had become public property and I wanted to take her back and let her be just ours again.

Then, as the autumn turned into winter, we were faced with the prospect of Christmas, Sarah's very favourite occasion. Everywhere I looked reminded me it was that time of year again: adverts on the telly, shop displays, school nativity plays. Usually the family loved the run-up to Christmas and preparations would begin weeks beforehand, with the children drawing up lists of presents for Father Christmas, decorating the house and tree, and making cards and biscuits. I would put an advent calendar up and they would take it in turns to open the doors and excitedly announce the number of days left until the big one.

Out of us all, Sarah loved Christmas the most. For her it was the magic of it: the elves, flying reindeers, Lapland, and Father Christmas coming down the chimney. On Christmas Eve it was always Sarah's job to hang up the stockings for Father Christmas to fill, and in the morning she would wake everyone up at the crack of dawn by jumping on the beds holding the full stockings. The year before she died, she woke us all at 4 a.m., and although we begged her for some more sleep, she wouldn't allow it. By breakfast time she had opened all her presents and declared her fairy-tale castle the best thing she had ever seen.

Christmas without Sarah was practically unthinkable. As December wore on I tried several times to open the box of decorations in the garage, but each time I went to open the lid I froze. Inside were cards and decorations that Sarah had lovingly made over the years and I simply couldn't bear to look at them, knowing the memories would be too much to bear. So the box stayed where it was and the house remained undecorated. If it had been only up to Mike and me, it would have stayed that way and we would have cancelled the whole thing. But of course we had the children to think about and they wouldn't let us forget.

It was the week before Christmas when Charlotte asked me, 'Why haven't we got a tree, Mummy?'

Looking at her sad little face I suddenly felt terribly guilty. 'Daddy and I haven't got round to it yet, darling, but we will,' I assured her, although I had no faith that we would.

'Do we still get presents this year? Father Christmas hasn't rung and asked what I want.'

With everything we'd had to think about, we hadn't arranged for Mike's brother to call the children and do his Father Christmas act.

'Daddy and I have told him what you want, sweetheart,' I said, although we hadn't bought a single present yet.

'Are we getting Sarah any presents?'

It wasn't something I'd let myself think about, but I knew the right answer instantly. As hard as it would be to buy her presents, it would be harder still not to.

'Of course we will.'

Having promised Charlotte a Christmas there was no getting out of it now, but the day before Christmas Eve we still hadn't got round to buying any presents or food, or decorating the house. As usual, Jenny and Ian saved the day. In the morning there was a knock on the door and there they were – Ian dressed up as Father Christmas holding a tree. Charlotte's face lit up as she saw him, and her reaction made me feel so guilty that we hadn't made any effort.

'Have you got your turkey yet?' Jenny asked me. I shook my head wearily. 'Thought not,' she said, 'so we got extra. You're all coming to us.'

'Are you sure, Jen? It's a lot of work for you.'

'Don't be silly, no arguments,' she said, and I gratefully accepted.

Ian had put the Christmas tree in the corner of the room and Charlotte was tugging at my jeans. 'Where's the decorations, Mum? I want to do the tree.'

I couldn't delay it any longer, so, with a heavy heart, I went and fetched the box of decorations, placing it in the middle of the living room floor and tentatively opening it. On the top were ragged bits of green and red tinsel, silver baubles, and gold stars which I picked out of the box and handed to Charlotte to drape over the tree. Underneath lay the things I was so afraid of. As the family bustled around decorating the room, I quietly sorted through mementoes from previous Christmases, lingering over Sarah's cards and drawings of smiling people opening presents, elves and pixies, and Christmas trees. Then, at the bottom of the box, there it was: Sarah's fairy. She had made it at school as a little girl and, every year since, Mike had lifted Sarah up so she could place it on top of the tree. This year she wasn't there to do it, so I reached up and placed it on the top branch myself.

Now we had a tree, but no presents to go underneath it. Taking charge, Jenny said, 'Right. We're going shopping.' Although it was the last thing I felt like doing, I didn't have much choice, as it would break Charlotte's heart not to have any presents to unwrap. Like most outings at that time, our trip into town was a disaster. We had grown used to being looked at everywhere we went, but people were usually quite subtle about it. For some reason, that day they weren't. We had barely stepped out of the car, when people started staring and whispering. One woman even spontaneously hugged me and said how sorry she was. Although I knew she – and everyone else – meant well, sometimes it was just too much to cope with. We ducked into Woolworth's to avoid the crowds, but there was no escaping the attention, as a woman in the CD section pointed straight at us and said to her friend in a loud voice, 'That's Sarah Payne's mum, the little girl that was murdered.'

Jenny saw me pale, and she lost her temper. 'You are SO rude,' she said to the surprised woman, and dragged me off by the arm.

'Can we go home now?' I asked Jenny.

'What about the presents?'

'I don't know. I'll get them tomorrow. I can't handle this today.'

So we went, leaving me with one day to buy the children their gifts. Thankfully, on Christmas Eve another friend came over and suggested driving me to Toys 'R' Us. That way, I could buy everything under one roof, minimising the time spent out of the house. I raced around the shop, buying Lee and Luke a stereo for their room and Charlotte a karaoke machine as their main presents, as well as some videos, computer games and clothes. The hardest thing was buying something for Sarah. I finally decided to buy the sisters matching dolls, and a beautiful stone angel for Sarah's grave.

On returning home, I found the children sitting quietly on the floor of the front room, paper and coloured pencils scattered around them.

'What are you drawing?' I asked.

'We're making cards for Sarah,' Luke replied, 'and look, I bought her a teddy with my pocket money.'

Seeing the little brown bear, I gave Luke a huge hug. Sometimes my children amazed me.

That night there was the ritual of hanging up the stockings at the ends of the beds, which had always been Sarah's job. Luke volunteered to take her place this year, and giving him three stockings instead of four was heartbreaking. As I tucked Sarah's away in a drawer it was so hard to believe that she would have no further use for it. Christmas morning was a subdued affair. With no Sarah to wake us, we got up in our own time. The children were pleased with their presents and Charlotte's stocking was overflowing, as I had subconsciously bought for two girls instead of just one, but the whole day just felt wrong without Sarah.

After breakfast we drove to the graveyard to wish her a happy Christmas, but as we approached the gates we were horrified to see several photographers holding cameras.

'Don't even think about it,' Mike threatened, as we drew level with them.

They were apologetic immediately. 'We're really sorry,' said one who I recognised. 'Our bosses made us come. We didn't want to.'

'I know you're only doing your jobs,' I said wearily, 'but not today, lads.'

'Just leave us alone,' Luke added, and we carried on walking.

Halfway into the cemetery I turned round. They were still there, but they didn't seem to be taking any pictures. Even so, just having them there made the whole experience even more difficult than it already was. At Sarah's grave, which still did not have a headstone as Mike and I simply couldn't find the appropriate words to write, we all said 'Happy Christmas' and I gave her the angel. Then Charlotte unwrapped Sarah's doll for her, telling her, 'I've got one too, but I'm going to keep yours safe for you.'

After we had been to the cemetery we went to Jenny and Ian's house, which was decorated from top to bottom and brimming with Christmas cheer. Before lunch the children went horse riding in the fields round the back, which was followed by the Queen's speech and a huge Christmas dinner with all the trimmings. When we were all full we played charades and Trivial Pursuit and polished off a few bottles of wine before it was time to go home. I can't say that the day was cheery exactly, but under the circumstances I think we all did well and we were grateful to Jenny and Ian for bringing us out of ourselves and not letting us dwell on things too much.

Sara and Mike on the beach where Sarah was playing before she disappeared,
and in the field from which she was abducted

The family releasing white doves at Sarah's memorial service at Guildford Cathedral

Sarah's coffin being carried by pallbearers at St Peter's church in Hersham

The family at Sarah's funeral

A schoolfriend of Sarah's from Bell Farm holding a purple balloon
on what would have been Sarah's ninth birthday

The family releasing balloons to mark Sarah's ninth birthday

Sara and Charlotte sorting through Sarah's Law petitions in the *News of the World* offices in Wapping

The family counting Sarah's Law petitions

Sara and Mike delivering Sarah's Law petitions to the Home Office

Sarah's Law press conference

The Pride of Britain awards

Sara and Carol Vorderman discussing child safety

The family today, including new arrival Ellie

5

SARAH'S LAW

One of the only things that distracted me from my misery in those months and gave me something to get up for in the mornings was the thought that we could do something to stop another family suffering as we were. I was determined that Sarah would not die in vain and it was from this desire that the campaign for Sarah's Law began. My daughter was gone and nobody and nothing could bring her back, yet as I agonised over her murder the thing that tormented me most was that it could have been prevented.

At first the family blamed themselves. Mike and I were guilt-ridden for leaving the children alone, while Luke and Lee berated themselves for not having caught up with Sarah as she left the field. But, with help from friends and professionals, we slowly came to accept that we were not to blame. The ultimate blame rested, of course, with whoever had done this terrible thing. Yet, as I talked to police officers, social workers and therapists, I came to realise that the system that deals with paedophiles and sex offenders also had to shoulder some responsibility.

The police knew as soon as Sarah's body was found that they were dealing with a predatory paedophile, a stranger who snatches children for their own perverse gratification. Whether or not it was Roy Whiting remained to be seen, but if it was not him it was someone similar. Like most ordinary people, at that time I knew next to nothing about paedophiles. I knew that they existed, as I had followed stories about the likes of Ian Brady and Robert Black along with the rest of the country. But I had no idea about their psychology or how they operated and I never imagined for a minute that such a person would touch my life directly. I naively assumed that sexual offences against children by strangers were incredibly rare and that when it happened the person was put in prison and never let out – or at least not until they were completely cured. I soon learned that this is far from being the case.

I was amazed to be told that, at the time of Sarah's murder, there were around 250,000 convicted sex offenders – nearly all men – living across Britain. Around 110,000 of those had committed sexual offences against children, and each year six or seven children are murdered in a sexually motivated attack. In a bid to curb the problem, in 1997 the government introduced the sex offenders' register to keep track of these people and monitor their activities. Unfortunately it was not backdated, so only around 12,000 people had signed up by the time Sarah died. I was also shocked to learn that the register relies on the offender's co-operation, requesting that he report to a police station and register his details when he is released from prison. Typically, around 97 per cent of offenders do register, which sounds a lot, but in actual fact 3 per cent not co-operating amounts to 360 sex offenders roaming around Britain unchecked. According to the NSPCC, over half of these people are a cause for concern and pose a danger of re-offending.

The crux of the problem is that there is simply no cure for paedophilia. Prison sentences for sex crimes against children are often short, and during the offender's time inside therapy and treatment are purely optional. Even when it is undertaken, rehabilitation is very rare. The general consensus among professionals who work with child sex offenders is 'once a paedophile always a paedophile'. It was explained to me that paedophilia is similar to any sexual preference – like being gay or straight – it is part of who someone is. You can no more 'cure' paedophilia than you can cure someone of being heterosexual or homosexual. Therefore, many paedophiles are genuinely convinced that they are doing nothing wrong. I was disgusted to hear that they claim to love children and say that relationships between children and adults are natural. Some are so deluded that they go so far as to claim that the children provoke them or want sex with them.

After paedophiles are freed from prison they may be able to keep their urges under control for a time for fear of going back inside. But eventually most cannot help returning to their old ways and 64 per cent of child sex offenders re-offend four or more years after their first conviction. A small number will kill the child – either to prevent being sent back to prison or as part of the perverted thrill. It seemed to me that the only way to protect our children was to lock the worst offenders away and never let them out. But even when life sentences are handed out, life does not mean life, and most are back on the streets in just over ten years.

Psychologists consulting on my daughter's murder said that whoever had killed her had probably committed offences before. The fact that he had managed to abduct, assault, murder and bury Sarah without any witnesses or visible clues suggested it was not his first time. Ray Wyre, a sex-crimes expert I got to know, also told me that the average paedophile will have abused over 200 children – with his crimes getting steadily worse – before being caught and prosecuted. So it was highly likely that Sarah's killer had struck before.

It seemed appalling to me that there were over 100,000 of these people living anonymously in our midst, watching and lusting after our children. If Mike and I had known that there was even one such person about we would never have left Sarah and the other children alone on the beach. But the sex offenders' register is not open to the public so we had no way of knowing. Surely those offenders who commit the most serious crimes against children – abduction, rape or murder – should never be let out of prison? 'Life' should mean life for them. For those convicted of 'lesser' offences against children, once freed they should not be able to hide. The public should be allowed to know who and where they are.

This train of thought triggered a memory of a television documentary that I had seen about a seven-year-old girl in America called Megan Kanka who had been snatched and murdered on 29 July 1994. Megan's killer was twice-convicted paedophile Jesse Timmendequas, who had previously served time for the sexual assault and murder of another girl. When he was released from prison he went to live opposite the Kankas' New Jersey home, but the community had no idea of his background as sex offenders' identities were protected by law. It was not until he raped, tortured and strangled little Megan that his terrible past came out. By then it was too late.

After Timmendequas's conviction Megan's devastated parents lobbied for changes in the law. They argued that if they had known that a paedophile lived on their street, they could have taken appropriate steps to protect their daughter, moving house or making sure she stayed away from him. Within 89 days of her murder, Megan's Law was introduced in the USA, giving parents the right to know about convicted sex offenders in their area. Introducing this new law, Bill Clinton called it 'a straightforward statement of morality and child protection'. I couldn't have agreed more and I wondered if such a thing could be done in England. Of course at that point I had no idea how we might go about trying to change the law, but the idea had been planted and I was waiting for a way to help it grow.

After Sarah's body was found the phone rang off the hook with press offers asking us to do exclusive interviews. We were offered sums of money up to £100,000 – for ourselves, the children, or a charity of our choice.

'It's sick,' Mike said. 'Do they really think we would accept money? It's like profiting from Sarah's death. I wish they'd just leave us alone now.'

'I know it doesn't seem right,' I said, 'but we do have loads of debts and it could be helpful for the children's future.'

'We'll manage,' Mike said. 'We always have.'

'All I'm saying is let's think about it,' I replied.

We sought the advice of Mike Alderson, who told us, 'I can't tell you whether you should or shouldn't accept any of these offers, but you should be aware of some potential problems. If you sign a contract with somebody it will mean that, for the first time since this has happened, you are exclusively bound to one newspaper or television programme. It's possible that other papers could take offence and things could get messy. Some people may also think badly of you for taking money.'

That sealed it. On the whole we had a good and mutually respectful relationship with the press and we didn't want to cause any bad feelings by seeming to favour anyone above anyone else. There was also a part of us that was scared about family problems being dredged up and our dirty washing being aired in public. So our minds were made up: there would be no exclusives, no money changing hands.

One of the many reporters to be in touch that week was Robert Kellaway from the *News of the World*, requesting an interview for that Sunday's edition. As I was explaining to him that we had decided not to do any exclusives or take any money, a thought came into my head and I suggested that he look into Megan's Law.

'If you have any ideas about how we might start something like that in Britain, then get back to me,' I told him.

Within twenty-four hours the *News of the World* had put together a proposal, and Rebekah Wade, the editor at the time, came to see us and suggested launching the 'For Sarah' campaign. The campaign would have two objectives. The first was to lobby for Sarah's Law, which would include a range of new measures to protect children. At the heart of Sarah's Law was the right of every parent to know about child sex offenders living in their area. To this end, the second part of the campaign was to 'name and shame' Britain's very worst convicted paedophiles so that the public knew who and where they were.

That day, Rebekah warned Mike and me that the campaign would be controversial and cause a big political and social stir, so we asked for a short amount of time to think about it.

Once we were alone in the kitchen, I said to Mike, 'It's a great idea, isn't it?'

Mike looked thoughtful. 'I suppose so.'

'Only "suppose"? Don't you think we should know where these people are?'

'Of course I do. I'm just not sure it's our place to get involved in something like this.'

'Why shouldn't we?'

'What do we know about politics? We're just an ordinary family.'

'It's not about politics, it's about family safety. And after what's happened, surely we're the most qualified people to talk about it? We can help, we can make a difference.'

'Maybe you're right,' Mike agreed.

I was determined that some good would come out of Sarah's death and, when I told Rebekah that we were 100 per cent behind the campaign, I firmly believed that we were acting for the good of every child out there.

The first Sunday of the campaign we went and bought a copy of the *News of the World*. Staring out from the front page was Sarah's picture, and above it was the bold black headline: 'NAMED SHAMED'. Inside the paper were the names and pictures of forty-nine paedophiles, along with the areas they lived in. Included in the article were quotes from us, and a stark warning against people taking the law into their own hands. We closed the paper, pleased with the article, and got on with our day. We had no idea what we were beginning.

Over the next two weeks all hell broke loose. The country was divided in its reaction: people were either passionate believers in the campaign or vehemently against it; there seemed to be no middle ground. On the one hand, the so-called 'ordinary British public' were overwhelmingly behind us. The *News of the World* office was swamped with phone calls, letters and e-mails from mums and dads supporting what we were doing; petitions for Sarah's Law were printed in the paper, which hundreds of thousands of readers signed; badges with Sarah's face on them with the slogan 'For Sarah' were made and sent out to people all over Britain; and a MORI poll found that 88 per cent of people questioned said parents should know if there is a paedophile living near them. Reading the messages of support we realised that we had really hit a nerve with the British public. People were sick of sex offenders' rights being placed above innocent children's, and it was time to do something about it.

Yet to our great surprise, the broadsheets, police, politicians and probation services all took a firm stance against naming and shaming. Campaign critics argued that exposing paedophiles would drive them underground, meaning that the authorities would no longer be able to monitor them. To this we answered: paedophiles are already underground. There are hundreds of offenders who do not comply with the sex offenders' register, simply disappearing into the night after their release. Those who do comply are inadequately monitored, as proved by the re-offence rate of 64 per cent. We knew that police and probation officers did their best, but they were simply terribly under-resourced. They cannot supply the twenty-four-hour monitoring these people need to keep them from re-offending.

Another worry was that the campaign would provoke vigilante action by incensed members of the public taking the law into their own hands. Ann Widdecombe, then shadow home secretary, even went so far as to say that the naming and shaming campaign was 'inciting a mob mentality'. Other MPs, including Colin Pickthall, were quick to agree, calling the campaign a 'very nasty witch-hunt, designed to appeal to the rabble-rouser, the violent and the just plain thick'.

Sadly, they were proved partly right. While most of the public reacted sensibly to the information we had given them, there were a few hot-headed people who misused it, targeting paedophiles and those they suspected of being paedophiles. In one case of mistaken identity, father-of-three Iain Armstrong's Manchester home was surrounded by an angry mob shouting 'paedophile'. After a brick was thrown through his neighbour's window, he had to have a panic button installed. The mob had mistaken him for Peter Smith, one of the paedophiles pictured in the paper. A group called Antimatter then surfaced, sending threatening letters to those they thought were paedophiles. Michael Horgan and Victor Terry were both wrongly identified and forced into hiding.

After a second week of naming and shaming in the paper, riots broke out in the Paulsgrove area of Portsmouth, where locals targeted the home of named paedophile Victor Burnett. This sex offender had been jailed for nine years in 1989 after his part in Britain's largest child sex ring. He had fourteen previous convictions and had abused a total of 140 children. After his release, Burnett had moved to Portsmouth, where he had spent three years in a flat just 50 yards from two primary schools. In the week after he was named in the paper, 150 protesters gathered outside his house. It started peacefully enough, but the protest soon descended into violence. Bricks were thrown, a car was torched, a policeman suffered a broken nose, and some of the mob smashed their way into Burnett's flat.

The naming and shaming campaign was directly blamed for the Paulsgrove riots and initially I was devastated. Watching it on television I broke down and cried to Mike, 'What have we done?' But we later learned the truth – the riots would have happened anyway. A few days after the problems started, the officers that policed the Paulsgrove estate came to see Mike and me. They visited ostensibly to bring a book of condolence for us, but their real reason was to tell us not to blame ourselves for what had happened. The Paulsgrove residents had learned about Burnett's convictions shortly before he was named in the *News of the World* and a demonstration had already been planned. At most, the paper was a catalyst.

Although I felt no sympathy for Victor Burnett, who was one of the worse predatory paedophiles in Britain, I knew that a civilised society cannot condone this sort of violence. When we heard of the vigilante attacks, particularly against innocent people, we felt sick and blamed ourselves. Sarah had been such a sensitive, peaceful little girl that we knew she wouldn't have wanted this. It was frustrating, as the hot-headed actions of a few were ruining the chances of Sarah's Law ever being passed, when we – and the paper – had specifically warned people against taking the law into their own hands. As far as we were concerned, vigilantes were criminals too and should face strict penalties, like they do in America.

In addition to the vigilante attacks, there were two suicides. Millionaire motorcycle dealer John Potter, wanted for questioning over indecent assaults on two fifteen-year-olds, shot himself at his home in Herne Bay in Kent. And James Oldham took an overdose after spending days on the run. There were also death threats to *News of the World* staff, Rebekah Wade was forced to get an SAS bodyguard, and a bomb scare evacuated the News International building.

We knew that we had to revise our initial strategy, as things were getting out of hand. We had to get back to basics. Our main aim was to keep children safe from paedophiles and we were still certain that the best way to do this was to give parents the right to know if there was a predator living in their area. We had been using the paper to do this, but ultimately this wasn't the right way to give people information. It needed to be done in a controlled and considered way by the proper authorities. The problem was that the naming and shaming campaign was alienating those we needed on our side the most: the police and probation services, the professionals who dealt with child safety issues on a day-to-day basis. We decided that if the proper authorities would back us and help fight for Sarah's Law, we would drop naming and shaming.

So, on Wednesday, 2 August, Mike and I attended a summit meeting with representatives from the *News of the World*, the Association of Chief Police Officers, the NSPCC, and the Association of Chief Officers of Probation, to see if some compromise could be reached. It was only a month after Sarah's death, and we were so raw that it took all our strength to get ourselves together to go. But, as much as we were hurting, it was the only positive thing we had to hold on to.

As the car pulled into the News International headquarters in Wapping, East London, there were camera crews and journalists swarming at the gates waiting to report the outcome of the meeting. There we met Stuart Kuttner, the *News of the World*'s managing editor, and Hayley Barlow, the public relations manager, and they led us up to the conference rooms. As we walked in, the various big-wigs were already sat around the oval table. There were so many agencies with so many acronyms that we could never remember them all, so Mike and I simply called them TESCOS for short. We took our seats and the discussion began.

The aim was to formulate a version of Sarah's Law that we all agreed on, but that proved easier said than done. What struck me immediately was how many egos were around that table. It was obvious that these people had never sat together in one room before and sensibly discussed child safety issues. They were all too busy fighting their own corners, for the interests of their own agencies, rather than working together for what was best to protect children.

Although everybody was sympathetic to Mike and me, we got the feeling that they slightly resented us being there. They clearly thought that they were the professionals and they knew better, but we weren't trying to upstage them or pretend we had all the answers. We didn't, but what we did have was common sense and terrible first-hand experience of how the system didn't work to protect children. When you stripped away all the bureaucracy it was simple. Our children were not being protected from paedophiles and that had to change. It seemed a great shame to me that they couldn't see that. At times I just wanted to give them a slap and tell them to get it together.

The meeting lasted four long hours. The police and probation services were desperate for us to drop the naming and shaming campaign, yet we were unwilling to do so without their support for Sarah's Law. In the end a compromise was reached, and a draft of Sarah's Law was drawn up for everybody to consider. After a two-day cooling-off period we agreed to suspend the naming and shaming campaign, and the police and probation services agreed to back Sarah's Law. It was a great feeling. We felt like we were really on our way to getting some serious changes made.

On 4 August a charter for Sarah's Law was drawn up that was agreeable to all parties. The campaign objectives were threefold. The first was to empower parents to protect their children from risks caused by sex offenders. The charter read:

> It is every parent's right to have controlled access to information about individuals in their neighbourhood, including convicted child sex offenders who may pose a risk to their child. In appropriate cases this access should be also given to responsible members of the public who have a responsibility for the care of children.
>
> There must be severe penalties for any person who abuses access to this information.
>
> Parents should be able to access a local record of all organisations to determine if their employees or volunteers are subject to the child access vetting procedures.
>
> Government should establish a task force to review

existing programmes to promote child safety for children and parents.

The second objective of the campaign was to empower victims of sex abuse:

When passing sentence, courts should have the power to prevent offenders contacting or living near their victims. The orders would be made on the basis of representations made by the victim.

Release licence conditions should include restrictions on contact with victims.

Every child victim of sexual abuse should as of right receive appropriate support, counselling and therapy.

The third objective was making prevention more effective:

The existing police vetting arrangements for people intending to work with children should be extended to cover all voluntary organisations. The government should make funds available to allow voluntary organisations to apply for the vetting information free of charge.

The existing sex offenders' register should be amended:

Registration would be required to be made within 72 hours.

The registration should be in person at designated police stations.

The offender should be required to have his or her photograph taken for identification purposes at the time of registration and at any other reasonable time when his or her appearance has changed.

The re-registration of offenders should take place at pre-determined intervals.

The penalty for failing to comply with the register should be increased from six months to five years' imprisonment.

Offenders should be required to notify foreign travel.

Sex Offender Orders should be revised to enable the police to make greater use of them as a proactive tool.

It is every victim's right to understand the sentence imposed by the court. Victims have a right to know what period in custody the offender will actually serve.

Sex offenders should be subject to a risk assessment process at the time of their sentence by the court and indeterminate sentences should be imposed in appropriate cases.

Where an offender is assessed as suffering from severe personality disorder and as a consequence poses a significant threat to children, he or she should be detained in secure accommodation.

With the charter agreed, we were now ready to take on the then Home Secretary, Jack Straw. A meeting was set up in September, between Jack Straw, Mike and myself, our local MP, and Rebekah Wade. As we walked into the House of Commons, Mike turned to me and said, 'I can't believe we're going to see the Home Secretary. I didn't even know his name until recently. It's madness.'

Before Sarah was killed I would have agreed with him – never in a million years imagining that I would set foot in such a place. I didn't kid myself that we were there on our own merits, because of who we were or what had happened to us. I knew that without the *News of the World* behind us we would be just another family outside waving banners. But the main thing was: whatever the reason, we were there, and we would do everything we could to make our voices heard.

I had built Jack Straw up in my mind to be some kind of great man, and as he greeted us pleasantly and said how sorry he was for our loss, I was uncharacteristically nervous, worried about being able to hold my own in a discussion with him. But as I started to put our case forward for Sarah's Law, telling him how it could have saved Sarah and could protect other children in the future, my nerves vanished. As I spoke, Jack Straw nodded sagely and made sympathetic noises, never agreeing or disagreeing with anything I said: a true politician. I then turned to the other changes that we were proposing, including better rights for victims and harsher penalties for offenders. On these less controversial subjects he was more forthcoming, saying that the government was actively working on some of the areas, and was willing to consider others. We were heartened to hear this, but when we tried to bring the discussion back round to controlled access to the sex offenders' register, again he shut down, saying only that more discussion was needed on the subject.

I came out of the meeting pleased that Jack Straw was considering some of the Sarah's Law proposals, but I still felt a bit flat. Yes, we had been to the House of Commons and Jack Straw had heard our case, but I didn't feel that he had really listened. I had been hoping that he would embrace the idea and take control of the situation, like politicians had done in the United States, but he had barely expressed any opinions at all. I couldn't even have a good debate with him. He was no different – no better, no worse – than me or Mike, or any of our friends and neighbours, apart from the fact that he had a high-profile, well-paid job. It was very frustrating, but if he thought that we were going to give up and go away, he was very much mistaken. We were determined to see this through.

Shortly after the meeting, Jack Straw announced a new package of measures to help protect children. In November the Criminal Justice and Court Services Act 2000 received royal assent, introducing amendments to strengthen the Sex Offenders Act 1997 and a new statutory system to stop sex offenders from working with children. Under the new laws, sex abuse victims must be informed when convicted paedophiles are to be released; judges can impose lifelong restrictions on convicted abusers and a breach is punishable with five years in jail; paedophiles must register with police in person within seventy-two hours of release, have their photographs and fingerprints taken, and notify police if they go abroad. Courts were also given powers to keep paedophiles away from their victims and ban them from places like schools and youth clubs. Maximum penalties for child pornography were increased and the age of those protected by the Indecency With Children Act 1960 went up from under-fourteen to under-sixteen.

It was a great start, and I was happy that the government was taking Sarah's Law seriously. But the Home Secretary still refused to agree to the central demand of Sarah's Law: parents' rights to controlled access to information about paedophiles in their area. In a letter he told us that such a register would not 'assist the protection of children or public safety'. As some sort of concession to us, the law was to be changed so that police could give information on child sex offenders to organisations working with children. Jack Straw told us, 'Controlled disclosure is a better and safer route. The police and probation services are the best placed to determine the disclosure of information.' But it wasn't good enough. There was no obligation on the police to give this information out; it was totally discretionary, so we vowed to keep fighting.

The next step was to take our campaign for Sarah's Law to the party political conferences. The first was the Labour Party conference in Brighton, where the *News of the World* had called a fringe meeting to discuss Sarah's Law. Before the meeting there were back-to-back interviews to be done – including BBC morning news, GMTV, the *Today* programme, local television and radio. As always, I preferred Mike to do the interviews with me, but I did my best not to put pressure on him. Often we would be in the green room, waiting to go on air, and at the last minute he would say, 'You go, I'll stay here.' I understood, but as I sat on the sofa alone in front of the cameras talking about our daughter, I missed his presence.

There were sixty or seventy people at the fringe meeting that afternoon and it was the first time that I had done any public speaking. Like the press conferences when Sarah was missing, I hadn't written down anything that I wanted to say. I found that when I did, I would get nervous about keeping to the script and things would come out wrong. I found it better just to be honest and speak from the heart. So I stood up and just talked: about Sarah, her murder, Sarah's Law. I was a bit shaky at first, but as I was speaking about something I passionately believed in I soon relaxed. Everybody in the room was either a mother or a father, a son or a daughter, and could empathise to some degree.

After I had presented our case the floor was opened up to a question and answer session. We had been prepared for some doubters, and we were not disappointed, but most of the criticism was aimed at the *News of the World*, rather than Mike and me. There were some people, inevitably, who thought that the paper had started naming and shaming as a cynical way to sell papers, but we knew this wasn't the case. The executives at the paper believed in Sarah's Law almost as passionately as us.

That night, a big group of us, including me and Mike, Terry and Les, and the *News of the World* team, went to a series of parties that were being hosted at the Grand and Metropole hotels where the conference was being held. It was a chance to network, to meet as many important people as possible and enlist their support. Dressed in our jeans and T-shirts, a glass of champagne in our hands, Mike and I stood out like sore thumbs, as we worked our way around the rooms, being introduced to politicians and newspaper editors. Superficially, we couldn't have been more different from them. We are a pint and game of pool type of couple who live on a council estate, and here we were surrounded by people who earned huge salaries and lived in plush houses. But at the end of the day we all had a common cause: keeping our children safe.

After a few hours of flitting from party to party, Mike disappeared. One minute he was there and the next he was gone. After ten minutes passed, I went upstairs to our room, where I found him lying on the bed, watching the television with a bottle of beer from the mini-bar in his hand.

'What are you doing?' I asked.

Mike looked up at me, and said in an agitated voice, 'I've had enough. I don't want to do this any more.'

'Do what?'

'Coming to places like this. Going on TV. I don't belong here and neither do you. I want to be at the Old House, standing at the bar with a pint and a fag, with our friends, not here swigging champagne. This isn't our world.'

'I know, Mike. I don't want to be here any more than you do, but we've got to carry on – for Sarah.'

'You carry on if you want. They don't care about me anyway. It's you they want.'

At these words I exploded in anger and screamed at Mike, 'That's not true. Sarah was your daughter too – not just mine. You loved her as much as me.'

'I know that,' shouted Mike, 'but they don't. They look straight through me. When they say how sorry they are about Sarah, it's you they're talking to – her mum.'

'Then show them. Show them you're as much a part of this as I am, by not giving up. You can't just stop now and leave me on my own. You're not being fair.'

'*I'm* not being fair? What's not fair is expecting me to go round smiling and shaking strangers' hands and talking about politics, when my daughter's been killed. I don't know how you can be so cool and calm. Sometimes it's like nothing's happened.'

At that point we heard a knock on the door, which stopped us in our tracks. Terry's voice called out, 'Are you both OK in there?'

We stared at each other for a moment, before I walked over and opened the door.

'Why don't you come back down?' Les asked. 'Have another drink?'

I looked at Mike, 'Come on . . .'

He sighed, 'Yeah, OK.'

We ended up going to meet the others at the Women in Journalism party. It was a bad move – I should have realised that Mike was at breaking point. After downing a couple of whiskies, he disappeared again. I went back up to the room, but he wasn't there, and I began to worry. As he had no mobile phone we couldn't reach him, so we all decided to split up and start searching. We spent the next couple of hours scouring the hotels, the sea front, and the pubs of Brighton. I kept expecting to find him propping up the bar of a proper pub, a pint in his hand, smoking a cigarette, but he wasn't anywhere to be found and in the early hours we had no choice but to give up.

The next morning he called. He had hitchhiked back to Littlehampton, where he had left the car, and then driven – several times over the limit – back home to Surrey. Now sober, we were both apologetic. Mike shouldn't have walked out and left me worrying about what had happened to him, but it was his way of making a stand and getting me to take notice of his feelings. Sometimes I got so caught up in what I was doing that I overshadowed him and didn't take his needs seriously. When this happened he would do something drastic to remind me that he was hurting too.

The next week was the Conservative Party conference in Bournemouth, where the *News of the World* had called another fringe meeting. Mike, understandably, was reluctant to go, but I thought it was important that we were both there. Eventually we reached a compromise: we would go to the fringe meeting and get our message across, but we wouldn't do any of the networking in the evening. The day got off to a bad start. The *News of the World* had sent a car to East Preston to pick up Mike, me, Terry and Les, but somewhere along the line there had been a mix-up and the driver went to Preston in Lancashire! By the time the mistake was realised and we had arranged a mini cab, we were running very late. When we finally arrived at the meeting, however, it was a great success. There were lots of members of the public there who supported us, as well as the usual mix of newspaper editors and politicians.

Afterwards we had a meeting with Ann Widdecombe. Like Jack Straw, she was very pleasant and sympathetic. At the end of the meeting she said, 'It was lovely meeting you, I'll certainly see what I can do,' but we got the feeling that she too was simply paying us lip-service and had no intention of going out of her way to fight for Sarah's Law. Sure enough, we later got a letter from her saying that 'we need to be cautious about the way we take this issue forward'. But as far as I was concerned, we needed to throw caution to the wind. I wanted change, and I would push until I got it.

6

ROY WHITING

Roy Whiting's name was first mentioned to us the weekend after Sarah went missing, and in the weeks and months that followed it cropped up with more and more regularity. The police were careful to keep an open mind and investigate all avenues, but privately they were sure that he had abducted and murdered our daughter right from the start. As soon as Sarah was reported missing, Detective Inspector Paul Williams, who kept track of local sex offenders, drew up a list of twelve paedophiles. Whiting came in at number one, and the police knocked on his door within twenty-four hours of Sarah's disappearance.

Whiting fitted the profile of the person they were looking for to a tee: he drove a white van, lived down the road in Littlehampton, and – most tellingly – had a previous conviction for the kidnap and sexual assault of a little girl. In 1994 he had abducted a nine-year-old off the street in broad daylight while she was playing with two friends. He bundled her into his car and threatened her with a knife, before driving her to a remote woodland spot, sexually assaulting her, and dumping her on the street. After police tracked Whiting down from the brave little girl's description, he eventually admitted the crime, saying he had just 'snapped'.

When I heard about Whiting's history I was incensed. The little girl he had attacked would bear the emotional scars for the rest of her life, yet Whiting was jailed for just four years after psychiatrist Anthony Farrington said he was not a paedophile, and Whiting promised that he would take part in therapy once in prison. He later changed his mind, not wanting the other inmates to know that he was a sex offender. The police told us that he even participated in a kangaroo court for paedophiles. As sex offenders cannot be made to take part in therapy, he simply served an extra seven months as penalty for his refusal. He was back on the streets in just over two years, with four months' supervision.

With this background, it was vital that police saw Whiting as soon as possible. The day after Sarah went missing, two officers turned up at his grotty little flat, where he lived alone, to question him. When asked what he had done the previous day he said that he had driven aimlessly down the coast, ending up at a fair in Hove. He claimed to have got home at about 8 p.m. – just after Sarah had been abducted – and been in bed by 9 p.m. He said he had been wearing a dirty white T-shirt that he had left in his van. Although they had nothing concrete, the police weren't happy with him, partly because of his manner. Some months earlier he had been questioned about two rapes in Brighton and he had been very relaxed and co-operative, because he had nothing to hide. Yet this time he was agitated and jumpy. He also stood out for his disinterest and lack of concern for Sarah, something even the most hardened sex offenders showed when questioned.

Because of their misgivings, the police decided to watch Whiting's flat. Thinking they were gone, a short while later Whiting emerged and walked to his white Fiat Ducato van, where officers saw him gather what looked like a bundle of clothes and take them inside. They called Detective Sergeant Steven Wagstaff, who arrived just in time to find Whiting sitting in the front of his van about to drive off. The detective blocked the van in and confronted Whiting, who was visibly shaking and nervous. Asked what he had taken out of his van, Whiting first answered tools, before changing his mind to socks, and then to a T-shirt. When police asked to see the T-shirt he had been wearing the day before, he produced a black one and then a sparkling clean white one.

The detective had to make the decision whether to let Whiting go – and hope that he might lead them to Sarah – or arrest him and seize the van. Without adequate resources to follow him, he decided to arrest Whiting and take the van in to be examined. He later said that it was the best decision of his career. If he had not, there is no question that Whiting would have found a way to dispose of his van – and with it all the forensic evidence that was later found there.

Whiting was taken to Bognor Regis police station and questioned by Detective Inspector Jeffrey Riley for a total of four hours over three days. Sitting slumped forward on his chair with his elbows on his knees, he answered each question with the same two words: 'No . . . com . . . ment.' Even when a police doctor found three recent scratches on his body he mockingly repeated the same words. It was his legal right not to reply, of course, but it was suspicious behaviour – particularly when there was a missing child involved. But although the circumstantial evidence against Whiting was mounting up, the police had nothing concrete to hold him on and they had no choice but to let him go. It was frustrating, but we had every faith in the police, knowing that if Whiting had done it they would find the evidence to put him away. We could only hope and pray that he did not harm another child in the meantime.

The police quickly set to work, removing 433 items from Whiting's flat and 302 from his van. In the back of the van, among the dirty clothes, rubbish and tools, the first suspicious items were found: some cable ties in the shape of handcuffs, which tightened when pulled together, a knife, a spade and a bottle of baby oil. It amounted to an abduction kit. Suspicions were also raised by the things that were not present in the van. When Whiting originally bought the Ducato it had a plywood floor and sides, and doors. By 2 July the wood panelling was missing and the doors had been changed – possibly to get rid of forensic traces. It was highly suspicious, but again not conclusive evidence. In a bid to get this, the scientists at Lambeth began conducting every forensic test known to man, doing DNA profiles on every stain on each piece of clothing. The work was very slow going, but they told us that if Whiting had murdered Sarah they would be able to prove it eventually.

On 17 July when Sarah's body was found and the case officially became a murder investigation, Detective Superintendent Peter Kennett replaced Alan Ladley as senior investigating officer. It was a huge investigation to take over, but Peter had a lot of experience dealing with major crimes. We liked him immediately. He was very professional and we had every faith in him, but he also had a quirky sense of humour that proved a welcome relief from all the heartache. A week after Peter took over, on 24 July, he had a lucky breakthrough when Whiting was arrested after leading police on a high-speed chase through Crawley in a stolen car and imprisoned for twenty-two months. This took some of the pressure off the police and bought them the time they needed to gather evidence without worrying about a possible killer being loose on the streets.

Then, on Monday, 31 July, after new evidence emerged, they arrested Whiting for the second time in connection with Sarah's murder after he appeared before JPs in Crawley on car charges. As he had been so uncooperative during questioning last time, a clinical psychologist and offender profiler were called in to give an assessment of the crime and offer police advice on questioning techniques. Whiting was interrogated again, with the officers focusing on new information that he had previously worked in Golden Lane, in Kingston Gorse, and still walked his dog in the field behind Terry and Les's house. But again he steadfastly refused to comment and was returned to prison, where at least he was in no position to harm another child.

Meanwhile, as good a suspect as Whiting looked, the police couldn't afford to concentrate on him and him alone. Police officers on the Yorkshire Ripper inquiry had learned this the hard way, blindly following a lead that turned out to be false, to the exclusion of all others. Peter Kennett told me that he would open the briefings the same way every day, asking, 'Does anybody know who did it?' When everybody chorused, 'No', he would then ask, 'What are we keeping?' and his officers would reply, 'An open mind.' Peter's way of operating was to try to disprove that Whiting had done it, rather than prove he had, searching for any evidence that might point to his innocence. There was none.

Five months into the investigation the breakthrough that we had been praying for finally came. Until that point nothing clearly implicated Whiting, but nothing pointed to his innocence either. In the run-up to Christmas, Peter invited me, Mike, Terry, Les, Dave, Sean and Martyn for a Christmas lunch at the George and Dragon pub at Burpham, near Arundel. It was always traumatic for us to go back to Sussex, but we hadn't seen the whole team together for a while, and it was Peter's way of saying that we hadn't been forgotten and were still very much part of the investigation.

We sat at the back of the pub, where we could have some privacy, overlooking the flooded fields, as it had been raining hard all day. As we were sipping our pints and ordering food, Peter's pager bleeped with a message to ring the incident room urgently. He called in immediately and one of the officers told him that Ray Chapman, the leading scientist, wanted to speak to him. When Peter got off the phone he was in a state of high excitement. Although he had spoken to Ray several times, apparently he had never called him before. 'I've got a feeling about this one,' he said, as he dialled Ray's office. 'I think it's going to be good news.'

Frustratingly, Ray was out at lunch and there was no mobile number for him. 'Bloody scientists,' Peter exclaimed, and we had no choice but to sit down to eat. We were meant to be having a long relaxing lunch, but now we were all on edge. As we tucked into our roast dinners and glasses of wine, Peter was jumpy, conscious that he could be on the brink of solving the case. Mike and I were calmer, as our hopes had been raised and dashed so many times over the past months. Eventually Peter got hold of Ray. 'I think we might have something,' started the scientist, and Peter took the mobile outside where he could hear better. When he came back, ten minutes later, he looked as excited as I had ever seen him, and we all fell into complete silence.

Sitting down and picking up his glass, Peter proceeded to explain to us exactly what Ray had said. Scientists examining the Velcro strip of Sarah's shoe – which had been discovered discarded in a field – had found 350 fibres, each of which were being compared to fibres from items in Whiting's flat and van.

It had taken some time, but they had finally found a match: microscopic red fibres found on Sarah's shoe were identical to red fibres on a sweatshirt recovered from Whiting's van. Two tests had already confirmed the match and Ray was confident that a third would prove it beyond all doubt. It was what we had been waiting for – evidence that established a concrete link between Sarah and Whiting.

It had been hard going to Sussex that day, but we were so glad we had. It was funny, but every time we all got together it seemed like something good happened. After explaining the new evidence, Peter told his officers to drink up. 'Sorry to cut this short, but we've got to get to the lab,' he said, and they rushed off to do their job, leaving me, Mike, Terry and Les to finish our drinks. There were mixed feelings around the table. Of course we were pleased with the news, but it also dragged us down, as contemplating the details of Sarah's death took us right back to the dark places that we tried to avoid. I know it sounds silly, as we all knew that Sarah had been murdered, but quite often we simply tried to think of her as having passed away. With every new piece of evidence, any glimmer of hope we had died. Our daughter had been murdered and we couldn't pretend that it hadn't happened. From there the dark thoughts were never far away. In our minds we were right there with her, going through her last minutes.

The new evidence was a great start, but Peter explained to us the next day that it might not be enough in itself. When Whiting bought the van there had been several items left in it and he could obviously say that the sweatshirt was one of them. This left us still needing more evidence and, just days later, we were given renewed hope when more forensic tests pointed towards Whiting. A blue fibre recovered from Sarah's shoe strap was found to match a clown-patterned curtain that had been recovered from

Whiting's van. After much research, police found that the curtain had been manufactured for Boots and was used in the stores that had baby changing facilities. The curtain was shown on *Crimewatch* and the girlfriend of the van's previous owner bravely came forward. She said that she had stolen the curtain from a Boots in East Grinstead and that was how it had made its way into the Fiat.

After months of nothing, luck was finally with us, as yet more forensic evidence surfaced. Shortly after Christmas two more red fibres from Whiting's sweatshirt were found among Sarah's hair. Then the final piece of the jigsaw fitted into place on the night of the police Christmas party in January. After Peter popped home to get changed, he got a call from the lead scenes of crime officer. On the red sweatshirt had been thirty hairs, twenty-nine of which gave no DNA profile whatsoever. The last one – a nine-inch blonde hair – gave a profile that stated that it was a one in a billion chance that it was *not* Sarah's hair. It was great news for the investigation – and for our peace of mind.

At this point, Peter told us, he stopped keeping an open mind. As far as he was concerned, there was no doubt: Roy Whiting had abducted and killed our little girl. Now Peter just had to convince the CPS that the evidence was strong enough to go ahead with a prosecution. Ever playing the fool, even in the most serious of times, Peter jokily told them that if they didn't prosecute Whiting he would arrest them and charge them with conspiracy to pervert the course of justice! Luckily it didn't come to that, as the CPS agreed that the evidence was strong enough.

Over the next few months, the case strengthened even more. Of the 200 fibres found in Sarah's hair, in addition to those from the red sweatshirt, eleven came from socks found in Whiting's van and one fibre matched the passenger seat front cover. When Sarah was moved from her horrible shallow grave her body had been put in a bag, which was later found to contain 400 fibres. One of these matched the driver's seat cover of the van, another matched the socks found in the van, and other fibres taken from a silver-coloured coat, which Sarah used to wear, matched blue fibres found in the right, front pocket of Whiting's jeans.

On 6 February 2001 Whiting was finally charged with the kidnap and murder of Sarah. Even then the only thing he had to say for himself was: 'No comment', the words often accompanied by a bored look and a yawn. After months of hoping, praying and investigating, we should have been elated, but the day that Whiting was charged was a bit of an anti-climax for everyone. Yes, it looked like Sarah's killer had been caught, but we still had a long way to go before he was behind bars for good. The fact that he had pleaded guilty in his previous case gave us some hope, but we were warned that he was unlikely to plead guilty to murder, as it would mean an automatic life sentence. There was the possibility he might plead guilty to manslaughter, claiming that he had not meant to kill Sarah, and the CPS would then have to decide whether to accept the plea or go for a murder conviction, which was a very tough decision.

Whiting was scheduled to appear at Lewes Crown Court on 19 February. Mike and I had never seen him in the flesh before, so we had no idea how we would feel when we finally clapped eyes on him, but we were determined to be there to stand face to face with him. We didn't want him to think that he had intimidated us into staying away. Any time that he stepped out of that prison we wanted to be there, watching him, not letting him forget what he had done to Sarah and our family. I wanted my face to haunt his dreams and nightmares like he had done mine, and to know that he wasn't going to get away with what he had done.

My mind was made up to go – but I was still terrified. When the day dawned I dressed in smart grey trousers and a white blouse, and pinned my 'For Sarah' badge to my jacket. As I tried to force down a piece of toast, I was suddenly overcome by a wave of nausea and I ran to the toilet where I was violently sick. I spent the next hour before we had to leave vomiting over and over again, the thought of seeing Whiting making me physically ill. Mike was just as apprehensive in his own way, sitting on the sofa shaking. Dave and Sean, who were driving us to Lewes that day, were both concerned about how Mike would react when he finally saw his daughter's killer, thinking that he might try to hurt Whiting. As we drove, they tried to keep the mood light. Dave said to Mike, 'Don't worry, if you do get to him we'll leave it a few seconds before we pull you off. And we've got our pepper spray.' I know it sounds in bad taste to be joking under the circumstances, but we found that it helped to keep us sane.

The main street in Lewes was jam-packed. Fifty extra police officers had been drafted in, in case there were demonstrations, and they were matched by an equal number of press, wanting pictures and comments. We didn't particularly want to, but we posed for pictures at the top of the steps, as the press had always been so good with us and we felt we owed them. Inside, once we had been through security, we were taken upstairs to an empty jury room, where we could be alone until the case was called. Terry and Les were there, as well as Mike's brother Paul and his girlfriend Zoe. Dave and Sean sat with us, as we waited nervously. After a few minutes, a lawyer for the CPS came and explained what was going to happen in court that day, before an usher popped her head around the door and told us it was time to go downstairs.

As we walked into the two-tiered courtroom, the first thing that hit us was how small it was. On the lower level was the dock, seating for the jury, legal teams, police and press, and limited public seating. Upstairs was the public gallery, which that day was packed with press. Whiting had not been brought up from the cells yet, but as we were led to our seats we were within touching distance of the dock. We were slightly shocked to be so close, but glad in a way, because as hard as it was for us, surely it would also be hard for him, having us so near? Dave and Sean sat on either side of us, hemming us in. They were still apprehensive that Mike might try to do something stupid, and wanted to minimise the chances of him succeeding.

Suddenly I felt Mike stiffen beside me and grip my hand tighter, and I looked up to see a man being led to his seat in the dock, flanked by three security guards. It was him: a middle-aged white man, with short hair, bad teeth, of average height and build, dressed scruffily in a grey T-shirt and black jeans. I blinked and swallowed. I don't know what I had expected, but not that. This man had killed our daughter and plunged our lives into chaos, and in our minds we had built him up into some kind of monster or devil. But he didn't have horns and he didn't look evil. Sitting there, hunched over, he just looked pathetic. At that moment everything he had become in my mind crumbled. I realised then that he was just a person. A sad, inadequate, pathetic man who I had no reason to be scared of.

As the proceedings started, and Whiting was called upon to confirm his name, I couldn't take my eyes off him for one second. I kept mentally willing him to turn his head and meet my gaze, but he never once even glanced at us. The hearing lasted just ten minutes. Whiting was asked not to make a plea there and then, but his solicitor, Gill McGivern, said, 'It is anticipated that "not guilty" pleas will be entered in due course.' She added that the defence would need months to prepare their case and would not be ready until the end of the year. As she said the words, Mike's grip on my hand tightened. It was the worst possible scenario: not guilty pleas, and months of waiting in limbo.

Whiting was then awarded legal aid and remanded in custody until 18 May. He actually yawned as the judge adjourned the case. It was the only emotion he showed through the proceedings – boredom. He never hung his head in shame, raised an eyebrow, or looked uncomfortable. He was just totally disinterested, sitting there with his arms folded. All along the police had said to us: he just doesn't care, he has no feelings of remorse about what he did. Up until we saw him for ourselves, we found this impossible to believe. How could you take a life – particularly of an innocent young child – and simply not care? But he didn't: Sarah's life meant nothing to him. We began to realise that nothing we could say or do would change that.

As court was adjourned Mike was shaking beside me and I knew that it was taking all his willpower not to do something stupid. I grabbed his hand and we fled the courtroom, not pausing to give any comment outside as we usually would. In the car on the way home Mike was agitated and I knew it was just a matter of time before his feelings erupted.

'How can that bastard plead not guilty?' he said. 'He knows he killed Sarah and we all know it too. What kind of a person could do that and then not even have the guts to own up to it? Why does he have to put us through this?'

'We don't definitely know he's pleading not guilty yet,' I said, trying to placate Mike. 'Let's just wait until May and see.'

But even as I said the words I knew they were hollow. None of us had really expected him to plead guilty. From his point of view, he had nothing to lose by going to trial. As we pulled up outside the house, Mike jumped out of the car. Sitting outside the house was our Savanna that we had driven the children down to Sussex in all those months ago. The car had three rows of seats and the children had always fought over who got the very back row. In the end the boys and the girls alternated when we went on trips. It had sat on the road since then, as Mike had not been able to bring himself to drive it. He had tried a few times, but every time he looked in the rear view mirror there was an empty seat glaring back at him. I think any reminder of Sarah would have set him off then, and it just so happened to be the car.

There was a metal bar lying on the front lawn and Mike grabbed it. I saw immediately what he was going to do and I shouted, 'Mike, no!' but he ignored me. Running up to the car, he swung the metal bar behind his head and smashed it against the side panelling, which caved in. He then took another swing, and another, and another, pounding away at the car, screaming his frustration. I stood at the side of the road looking on helplessly. The neighbours were peering out of their windows and people on the street were casting nervous glances in our direction, but after my first shout I didn't attempt to stop him. There was no point. He needed to do it. After the bodywork had been smashed to bits, he started on the windows, and the windscreen, until there was glass and chips of paint all over the road. He then dropped the metal bar and started kicking the car. He was hurting his feet more than the car by that point, but he couldn't stop until he had worked his frustration out.

Finally, he was spent, his energy completely drained, and he collapsed to the floor and sobbed like a baby. Only then did I go over to him and put my arms around him and gently lead him back into the house, where he sat and cried and cried until there were no more tears left in him. Later, when Mike had calmed down, we managed to see the funny side as usual.

'You looked like Basil Fawlty beating the Austin 1100 with a branch in *Fawlty Towers*,' I told him, with a smile on my face.

'I don't think he did as much damage as me though,' Mike said laughing.

'Never mind. We couldn't use it anyway. Easy come, easy go,' I shrugged.

7

THE PRIDE
OF BRITAIN

One morning in April 2001, I woke from a fitful sleep with my
hand under the pillow holding the red and black checked woollen
shawl that had been my daughter's comfort blanket. It had
accompanied Sarah everywhere when she was alive, and I now
slept with it every night. As I lay there that morning I wished for
the hundredth time that it had never been cleaned, as Sarah's
scent had gradually faded over the ten months since she had
been taken.

Still groggy from sleep, I automatically reached over and
turned off the alarm clock, which had not yet rung. For a few
hazy seconds, everything seemed as it should be. The clock
showed just gone 7.30 a.m., the spring sunshine filtered through
the curtains, and Mike was warm next to me. Through the thin
walls of our house I could hear the children bickering quietly.
Charlotte wanted to play Mario Brothers on Lee's PlayStation
before school, but he wouldn't let her. It was a common argument
between them. I lay there listening, with a smile, unconsciously

waiting for Sarah's voice to pipe up, loudly supporting her sister, as she always did. But, of course, the voice never came and it never would, and I was brought down to earth with a bump.

Sarah had always been the most bubbly and noisy of our four children, maintaining a stream of incessant chatter. There was never a quiet moment with her around, bounding in after her dance class, singing SClub7 songs at the top of her little voice, then pleading with us over and over to buy her their new CD, or performing fashion shows to music. Even when she was doing quiet activities, like drawing pictures of people doing handstand races, she would hum or chatter away. We were constantly telling her to pipe down, worried that the neighbours would be disturbed by her shrieking through the thin walls. Now I couldn't believe that we had ever told her to be quiet, as the house was so still without her.

I dragged myself out of bed and pulled on my pink and white dressing gown. Leaving the bedroom I nearly tripped over the dirty laundry that had been strewn at the top of the stairs for two days waiting to be washed. I noticed, without really registering, that Sarah's green chenille polo-neck jumper had found its way into the pile yet again. It constantly turned up, along with various other bits that Charlotte had squirrelled away, although they didn't fit, or suit, her. Downstairs, the kitchen was a mess, with dirty plates left in the sink, take-away wrappers and empty Fosters cans littering the worktops. Our dog, Fifa, was barking, demanding to be let out or fed, I couldn't work out which. Realising that I had a headache from too much to drink the night before, I made a cup of black coffee and swallowed two paracetamol, before returning upstairs.

I noticed gratefully that the children seemed to have resolved their differences and were playing quietly in the boys' room. Stepping into the shower I shivered under the cold water. With such a big family the hot water never lasts long. Soaping and rinsing myself quickly, I picked up a towel from the floor and dried off. I walked back into the bedroom, which was still only half decorated from the recent move, mismatched wallpaper peeling off the walls. Sitting on the bed, I nudged Mike, who was buried under the covers.

'Time to get up,' I said.

'Do I have to?' he groaned, and rolled over, wrapping the duvet tighter around him.

I decided to give up for the time being. Off the back of a chair I picked up a pair of blue jeans and a T-shirt – my usual uniform. I couldn't find any clean socks, so helped myself to a pair of Mike's. In front of the mirror I brushed my long hair, which was still damp from the shower. Like most days, I went without make-up. Mike and I have always dressed casually, and didn't see why we should change now, just because we were in the public spotlight.

I knew Mike was delaying getting up as he was dreading the day ahead. We were travelling to London for the *Mirror*'s Pride of Britain awards, where ordinary people who had shown particular courage or determination over the past year are honoured. The award winners were nominated by *Mirror* readers and selected by a panel that included Richard Branson, Simon Weston, Lord Winston, Denise Lewis, Richard Madeley and Judy Finnigan. The event was taking place over two days, and ended with an award ceremony with 100 VIP guests including the Prime Minister. Mike and I had been chosen to receive a 'Special Award' for our work campaigning for Sarah's Law – the right of every parent to know if there is a paedophile living in their area.

Going into the boys' room, I herded the kids downstairs for their breakfast of Frosties and toast. The night before I had explained to them that Mike and I were going away for a couple of days. When I told them that we were getting an award, Lee and Luke seemed proud, but Charlotte was too young to understand. Her first response was, as always, 'Can I come too?' Her next question was just as predictable: 'Why not?' But once she understood that Auntie Fiona was to be looking after her, she brightened up no end as Fiona was like a second mum to the kids, having been around since they were born. As we ate, my mum poked her head around the dining room door. She had slept on the sofa the night before, as she was coming to the awards ceremony with us. She had been to have her hair styled and was smartly dressed in a knee-length skirt and blouse.

'Morning, love, ready for the big day?' she smiled.

I hadn't seen her so animated – and proud – since before Sarah went missing and I promised myself that we would try to be upbeat, if only for her sake.

Mike finally surfaced, and as he came down the stairs I saw that the bags under his eyes were even more pronounced than usual. He said good morning to the kids, leaning down to give Charlotte a kiss, and put the kettle back on. Meanwhile, the usual last-minute school panics began. Luke didn't have a pen, Lee needed dinner money, and Charlotte couldn't decide which shoes to wear. As we looked in the shoe rack by the front door I flinched as I noticed Sarah's dark blue trainers sitting there. They looked so tiny, as Sarah only had size 13 feet when she died. Normally her shoes only lasted two or three months as she was quite hard on them, but these had lasted ages, as she was too girlie to wear them often. It's funny, the trainers get moved around, people clean them, but they always end up back in the rack. There never seems like a right time to throw them away.

I walked Charlotte to school, as I always did, giving her an extra big hug and whispering 'I love you' before she ran into the playground. My heart was heavy, leaving her, but when she looked back at me, with a wave and a smile, I knew she would be OK. I then headed home where I packed a bag with two changes of clothes, for dinner that night and the ceremony the next day.

A black Mercedes – courtesy of the organisers of the awards – pulled up outside the house at 10 a.m. The idea was that the families being honoured were treated like kings and queens for the day. On our estate the sight of a car like that was enough to start curtains twitching and I knew what the neighbours would be thinking. There were people locally that thought our lives were so much better now that Sarah was dead, as if a chauffeur-driven car, fancy hotel or bottle of champagne could make up for her loss. They also assumed we had taken vast sums of money from the media for interviews. They never said it to our faces, but friends of ours would get into arguments at the post office and bus stop, after overhearing people gossiping.

On the drive to London from Surrey there was a definite tension between Mike and me, but Mum chattered away excitedly. Apparently Joan Collins was attending the awards and Mum was dying to get a good look at her. She couldn't believe that someone of nearly seventy – five years older than her – could still look so youthful. At midday we pulled up outside the four-star Cumberland Hotel in Marble Arch, a huge white building overlooking Hyde Park. The chauffeur jumped out to open the doors for us, and another uniformed man appeared as if out of nowhere to take our bags, and we were whisked inside like royalty. In the foyer we were met by representatives from the *Mirror* newspaper, who explained to us the format of the next two days, which started with a get-to-know-you dinner that evening and finished with an award ceremony at the Hilton the next day. For now, we had the afternoon to ourselves.

A hotel porter showed Mike and me to our room, and Mum to hers. The room, with its king-size bed and feather pillows, over-stuffed armchairs, mini bar and television was a far cry from the sort of places we were used to staying in. Before Sarah's death, we wouldn't have been caught dead in a place like that – it just wasn't us. We were more at home in a caravan. We felt we were being ungrateful – not appreciating the nice things that people were doing for us – but after Sarah's murder we seemed unable to feel any real happiness or excitement about anything, like the gloss had been taken off life.

So, rather than enjoy the room, we hit the hotel bar for our first drink of the day. Mum and I settled down at a table in the corner, while Mike went to the bar and ordered two pints of Fosters and half a bitter. We had hoped that the dark corner would provide us with some cover, but we were recognised almost instantly. A smartly dressed young woman casually glanced in our direction, looked away, and then did a double-take. As she looked again I could see her eyes filled with sadness and pity. She gave me a weak smile, which I returned, and I could almost see her battling with herself, deciding whether to come over and say something. I was grateful when she didn't.

It's always difficult in these situations, because the public helped us so much in our search for Sarah. When we were doing the first appeals we shared everything with them because we wanted the public to feel that Sarah was theirs. We reasoned that if people felt personally involved they would be more likely to come forward with any information. Since we had given the nation ourselves and Sarah, and they had taken us to their hearts, it would be wrong to ignore them now. Yet there were times when I wished I were invisible.

That day we had intended just to have one or two drinks to relax. But, like most days, our good intentions quickly went out the window. After a couple of halves of bitter, Mum went up to her room to rest before the evening's dinner, and Mike and I stayed at the bar. We thought about ordering a late lunch, as we hadn't eaten all day, but in the end decided to forgo food for more drinks. By the end of the afternoon we'd had seven pints each. That amount of alcohol would make most people feel quite drunk, but it showed how far we'd come that I barely felt it.

With an hour to go before dinner, we went upstairs to get our glad rags on. I changed out of my jeans into my posh dress, which was floor length with a bodice and spaghetti straps, in a two-tone blue. My hair, as usual, was long and down. I was uncomfortable in what I called my 'girlie gear', but as my lipstick and foundation made a rare appearance, I resolved to be positive. Mike was having a harder time. He reluctantly pulled on a pair of trousers and a shirt, before opening the mini bar and selecting a miniature bottle of Scotch. All the time we were getting changed he had been silent, but now he turned to me.

'Do we have to do this?' he asked. 'It feels all wrong. It's like we're getting an award for our daughter being murdered. We're not brave, we haven't done anything special, we've just muddled through as best we can, like any parents would do.'

I paused, then said, 'I know what you mean, but we're here now. Let's just do it.'

He looked like he was about to argue the point, but instead just sighed, nodded his head resignedly, and knocked back the Scotch.

Downstairs in the dining room were four long tables, laid with white china, silver cutlery, wine glasses and name settings. Mike, Mum and I were sat together, along with newspaper astrologer Jonathan Cainer, who Mum started chatting to immediately. She and I have always been believers, whereas Mike is a definite non-believer. I reached for the nearest bottle of white wine and filled our glasses and Mike rolled his eyes as Jonathan explained the position of the planets to Mum.

At the front of the room Carol Vorderman stepped up to the stage. I had met her before, as she was a vocal campaigner for the safety of children, particularly with regard to the internet. She took the microphone and the room fell silent as she greeted everybody and explained what the awards were about. As our prawn cocktail starter was served, she started introducing the nominees. We were among the first.

As Carol said our names, we stood up. 'I'm sure you all recognise Sara and Michael Payne,' she began, and explained that we were nominated for a 'Special Award' for the campaigning we had done for Sarah's Law. The rest of the nominees clapped politely, and we sat down again to listen to the other stories.

A woman called Jill Farwell stood up. Carol explained that she had raised over £4 million to set up a hospice in North Devon for children with terminal illnesses, after her daughter Katie and son Tom both died of a rare degenerative disorder. Next out of their seats were PC Daran Gagin, of Leicestershire Constabulary, and PC Ian Thomson, of British Transport Police. They had rescued a would-be suicide victim by clinging on to him from a signal gantry above a railway track five miles from Leicester station. There was applause, and then electrician Brian Krishnan rose to his feet. He had saved two children from their blazing home in Surrey. Next was Dr Rosemary Radley-Smith, a paediatric cardiologist, who had set up Chain of Hope, bringing chronically ill and poor children from developing countries to Britain for vital treatment. And taxi driver Michael O'Leary, who averted a major disaster on a motorway when another motorist suffered a heart attack and fell unconscious with his foot lodged on the accelerator.

Then there were the children: eight-year-old Jamie Baxter saved his mother's life when she collapsed into a coma at their Northumberland home; three-year-old Connor Carr dialled 999 when his mother collapsed with an epileptic fit at their home in Tyne and Wear; twelve-year-old Katie-Louise Beynon revived her seven-year-old brother when he suffered a potentially fatal reaction to his asthma medication. And so the list went on.

Hearing these stories of courage, I became increasingly agitated. These people had saved lives, they had dedicated years to good causes. Mike was right, we weren't brave or courageous like them, we hadn't done anything to be commended for. We had been thrown into a nightmare and lived through it. I felt like a fraud even being among these people. I looked over at Mike and I knew he was feeling it too. I also knew that he was drunk. Mike is usually fairly quiet around people he doesn't know, unlike me and my big mouth, always ready to jump in and give an opinion. But the drink makes him louder and a little obnoxious. I knew there was going to be trouble when I overheard him telling Jonathan Cainer that astrology was all 'a load of old rubbish'.

With the introductions finished everybody got up to mingle, and that's when the problems really started. I heard raised voices from the other side of the room and, looking over, I saw Mike having a heated argument with another man, who I didn't recognise. Striding over, I surveyed the scene. Mike was flushed from the drink, the top buttons of his blue shirt were undone, and he was slightly wobbly on his feet. Apparently he had made an inappropriate comment about a female reporter's figure, and her friend had pulled him up on it, telling him to treat women with more respect. Mike threatened to punch him, and just as the argument looked set to come to blows, a girl started crying loudly. It was Joanne Harris, the girl with Down's syndrome who Craig from *Big Brother* had donated his £70,000 prize money to for a heart and lung transplant. She had taken a shine to Mike earlier in the evening, giving him big cuddles, but now his behaviour was scaring her and she had tears streaming down her cheeks.

The loud crying just served to wind Mike up even more and, just like that, he lost it. With a wild, desperate look on his face, he shouted, 'I don't want to be here,' so loudly that his words seemed to reverberate around the room. Realising that people were looking at him, he turned to storm out. Again, I made a grab for his arm, pleading with him to calm down.

'You can't just walk out,' I implored. But he pulled away and stomped out into a side room, with me at his heels.

Tears streaming down his cheeks, he choked, 'I can't do this. I've told you before but you won't listen, I can't deal with the press and the public, it's too much. I feel like I'm going mad. I need to be by myself.'

Trying to be rational, I told him that we could talk about it when we got home, but that now we were here we should go through with it.

But Mike was beyond reason. In his frustration he kicked out, making contact with a twelve-foot-high plate glass window. The noise of it shattering was deafening and stopped us in our tracks. We looked at one another wordlessly, wondering what to do next. A security guard was there within seconds, and seeing him Mike ran. Instinctively, I ran after him, ignoring the people spilling out of the dining room to get a good look at what was going on.

Mike made a dash out of the front of the hotel, on to the street, with me chasing after him, shouting, 'Mike, it's OK, come back.'

My long dress and high heels were slowing me up, but I finally caught up with him and tried to pull him back towards the hotel.

He shook me off angrily, screaming, 'I'm not going back there, I can't, I've had enough.'

People on the street were turning and staring at us, dressed in our evening wear, shouting at each other, but we didn't care. When I realised that Mike wasn't going to come back, I suggested that we take a walk. As neither of us knew London we just started to walk in a straight line, away from the hotel.

As we walked, we argued, shouted, screamed and cried. 'I'm sick of seeing us every time I turn on the TV or read a newspaper,' Mike sobbed. 'I can't take any more pictures and interviews. I just want to get on with my life. I want things to be like they were. I want everything to go back to normal.'

Seeing Mike in such a state, I was suddenly overwhelmed with guilt. This was something he'd tried to make me understand before. Trying to comfort him, I said, 'If you feel that strongly about it, then it's OK, you don't have to do any more work with the press about Sarah or the campaign, I can do it myself.'

But that only incensed him further: 'She's my daughter as well,' he exploded. 'It's always "Sarah's mum this, Sarah's mum that". I know you were her mum, but I was her dad, and I miss her so much I can't stand it.'

'I know . . .' I began, but Mike cut me off.

'I've got to go,' he said, 'I just can't do this. Go back to your mum, let's speak tomorrow.'

And with that he ran and hailed a black cab. Suddenly I was by myself. As I watched Mike's cab pull away I was fighting different impulses. Part of me was tempted to jump in a cab and follow him to make sure he was all right. But another voice told me that he was a grown man and had a right to be alone. Besides, my mum would be worried about me, and I would be letting a lot of people down if I simply ran away.

Having decided to go back to the hotel, I realised that I had no idea where I was or how far we had walked. In my rush to get out of the Cumberland I had left my handbag, so I didn't have any money to get a cab or my mobile with me to phone anyone. I considered flagging down a cab and getting someone to pay at the hotel, but I quickly rejected the idea. I was embarrassed by what had happened and didn't want to face people quite yet. I turned around and started walking back in the direction we had come from, hoping that we had just walked straight.

As I calmed down, I started to realise that I was cold and my feet were killing me. There wasn't much I could do about the weather, but I crouched down and unbuckled my shoes, slung them over my shoulder, and started to walk in my bare feet. The streets were dirty and cold, but that was the least of my worries. After I had walked about half a mile, lost in my thoughts, I approached a big group of young men, swigging from beer bottles, smoking, making jokes. Head in the air, I strode confidently through the centre of the group, to whistles and cat-calls. I gave them a hard stare and carried on walking.

Just as I passed the gang, a car pulled up to the side of the road and the driver wound down his window. At that instant my stupidity hit me: after everything that had happened, what was I doing walking around a strange city alone in the dark? Not breaking pace, I strode ahead and refused to look at the car, thinking he might just go away. Then I heard a voice, 'Are you OK, love? Can I give you a lift anywhere?'

It was a kind voice, and I looked over to see a big black man with a wedding ring on his finger and a gentle face, driving an expensive four-wheel drive. In the back of the car were two child seats. He looked genuinely concerned for my safety, but after what had happened to Sarah I was wary, so initially I said, 'Thanks, but I'm fine.'

'I understand,' he said. 'What about if I just drive next to you and make sure you don't get into any trouble?'

I didn't realise it then, but the man had recognised who I was. We talked like this, me walking, him driving, for ten minutes or so, until the cold made me relent and gratefully climb in the car.

As we pulled up to the hotel, the man turned to me and said, 'I just want you to know that I know who you are and what you're fighting for and I'm behind you 100 per cent.'

I thanked him and walked slowly into the hotel, where my mum was waiting. 'Mike's gone,' I shivered. 'I'm sorry.'

'Don't be silly,' she answered, putting her arms around me for a cuddle. 'You're cold,' she added, rubbing my back to warm me up.

The hotel manager walked over with some representatives from the *Mirror*, who were quick to reassure me that everything was OK. They told me that the window was being fixed and I shouldn't give it a second thought. I was grateful that nobody was making a fuss. In need of some comfort I did what came naturally – I went to the bar. Over the course of the day and night Mike and I had probably had around fourteen pints, three bottles of wine, and a few shorts each. And as I held my drink I had no doubt that wherever he was now, he had one in his hand too. It sounds like a lot to drink, but however much we had it only took the sharp edges off life, it was never enough to make us forget.

As I relaxed, exhaustion set in and I kissed Mum and went to bed. In the room I pulled my dress over my head, replacing it with a white dressing gown. I wiped my make-up off in the bathroom and tied my hair back from my face. It was late – after 2 a.m. – and I got into bed, pulling the sheets and blanket over me. Mike's clothes were still scattered across the room and the bed seemed even bigger without him in it. I knew that I wouldn't be able to sleep without speaking to him, so I rang our home number. The phone rang and rang, and just as I was on the verge of hanging up, Mike answered, his voice thick with sleep and booze.

'Are you OK?' I asked.

There was a pause, then, 'I don't want to talk now. Let's speak tomorrow.'

And he hung up.

I knew that this was a crucial point for us – we had reached the stage where something had to give or we wouldn't have a marriage left. Mike had always been uncomfortable dealing with the media. He hated being under the microscope all the time – he felt he was stepping into a world he didn't belong in. He had come this far with the campaign because he believed in Sarah's Law, but he couldn't handle the pressure any more.

The worry for us was that if he gave up his public part in the campaign and I carried on, people might think he didn't care. I had always been the more vocal one out of the two of us, the spokesperson for the campaign, simply because I am more comfortable with public speaking. So he sometimes felt like a spare part. The last thing I wanted to do was alienate him any more. I knew that if I pushed him too far I would lose him, and after so many years together I couldn't face life without him. This meant I had a choice: I could carry on alone, or drop the whole idea. I didn't sleep that night, going over things in my head, and texting my best friend for advice.

In the morning, I rang Mike. The conversation was brief, but better than the previous night's. 'How are you this morning?' I asked him.

'A bit better. I'm sorry about last night, I just couldn't do it. Was there trouble about the window?'

'Don't worry, it's all sorted, they were really nice about it. As long as you're all right, that's the main thing.'

'Yeah, I am, you stay there and get the award, I'll see you later.'

Stepping in the shower, I felt so weary. I just wanted the day to be over. I couldn't muster any enthusiasm for the awards any more. I didn't want to be in a glitzy hotel with celebrities, I wanted to be back with Mike in our house, watching telly and playing with Charlotte. It was a mistake to have come. It was too early for us to be doing things like this, we were still too raw. But I couldn't back out now. I had to put on a brave face.

After washing away the remnants of yesterday, I dried myself on a fluffy white towel, and dressed for the awards. My chiffon dress was knee-length and black with a pattern of purple and white flowers. I teamed it with black tights and high heels, applied concealer under my eyes to hide the dark circles, and added black eyeliner and mascara. As I stepped out of the lift into the foyer, the first person I saw was Carol Vorderman, who was hosting the awards. Dressed in a pair of black trousers and a bright orange silk shirt, she gave me a big smile and laughed, 'Bloody men, eh?'

I was so grateful to her, as her comment immediately took away the embarrassment I felt about the night before. I smiled and rolled my eyes. 'Tell me about it.'

Mum appeared then, looking pretty in a matching skirt and jacket, made from black and blue silk. She didn't even mention the previous night's events. Her motto has always been, 'Least said, soonest mended'.

With the events of the night before forgotten for now, we were whisked off to the Hilton on Park Lane. Before dinner and the award ceremony there was a champagne reception. As well as the award winners, there were celebrities everywhere we looked, all dressed up to the nines: Geri Halliwell, Vinnie Jones, Ulrika Jonsson, Cilla Black, Joan Collins, Mick Hucknall, Melinda Messenger, and many more. We chatted with Charlie

Dimmock about gardening for a while, and Mum was happy to get a glimpse of Joan Collins, amazed that she really did look as young in the flesh as she did on television. But while I was grateful that all these stars were lending their support to the event, I thought it was important that we remembered whom the night was really for. I greeted several people I'd met the night before and also met war hero Simon Weston, who I had always admired.

The pre-dinner reception was only meant to go on for half an hour, but an hour later we were still there, getting increasingly tipsy on champagne. We were waiting for the Prime Minister and his wife to arrive for photos, and they were running late. When another half-hour slipped by and there was still no sign of the Blairs, I began to get annoyed. We weren't allowed into the dining room before they arrived, and there were a lot of children at the event, who were getting hungry and fidgety. I thought it was bad manners to keep so many people waiting.

Finally, Tony and Cherie Blair arrived. Before the photos were taken, the Prime Minister went round the room shaking hands. When he neared me, I stepped forward and put out my hand.

'I'm Sara Payne, I've been wanting to meet you,' I said.

He didn't say a word, just smiled at me in an abstract way, shook my hand, and turned away. I knew that he was aware of exactly who I was and I was angry but unsurprised by his attitude. Despite massive support from the British public, the government remained steadfastly opposed to Sarah's Law. I suppose that he didn't want to be put on the spot about it in front of so many people.

After a group photo, we were finally ushered into the dining room, where there was seating for around 200 people. Mum and I were sitting with Bill Roach, who plays Ken Barlow in *Coronation Street*, and his wife. Tuxedoed waiters filled our glasses with wine, and we chatted easily until Carol Vorderman took the stage.

'Welcome to the *Mirror*'s Pride of Britain awards,' she smiled. 'In the room with us today is an extraordinary group of people. They are the unsung heroes of Britain, individuals who, when faced with disaster or with the odds stacked against them, have responded with courage and with dignity. We are here to meet the modest and the inspiring. The people who make Britain what it is today.'

The audience gave a warm round of applause before the Prime Minister stepped to the podium. 'Ladies and gentlemen,' he began, 'It is my very great pleasure to be here at the Pride of Britain Awards.' He continued, 'I hope that through the stories you hear today, the remarkable stories of remarkable people, perhaps ordinary people but in extraordinary circumstances, we get a sense not merely of what is best about this country, but what can be best about its future too.'

It was now the turn of the winners to be introduced. A projector screen flickered to life behind Carol, and for each award there was a video outlining the circumstances that led that person to be there. Although we all knew each other's stories from the night before, seeing the re-enactments or news footage screened was very emotional for everybody. Looking around me I could see people wiping their eyes and putting comforting arms around each other. Finally, mine and Mike's names were read out. At that moment I wished more than anything that he was by my side, holding my hand under the table.

'Last year the tragedy which bought our nation together was the murder of Sarah Payne,' Carol began. 'When Sarah was abducted the whole country wished and hoped for the news that she would be found alive and well. That news never came. Since that time Sarah's mum and dad, Sara and Michael, have campaigned to protect other children from the fate which their daughter suffered.'

The screen lit up and footage from a press conference we had done all those months ago when Sarah was still missing appeared. It was set on the beach in Littlehampton, where Mike and I had taken the kids just hours before Sarah was snatched. As I watched my anguished face on the screen and heard myself begging for Sarah's safe return, I burst into tears. Beside me, Mum did the same. We had been going through hell that day, but at least there had still been hope. Now there was none.

Mum squeezed my hand, as the screen was suddenly filled with Sarah's school photograph, in her little red jumper, the picture that had been on the front page of every newspaper from the day she had disappeared until the day she was found. Then, in a shocking contrast, the video flicked to pictures of Sarah's little body being removed from the field where it had lain in a shallow grave for seventeen days. I closed my eyes briefly, and when I reopened them my family and I were placing lilies at the spot. Lastly, the campaign for Sarah's Law was introduced, and a picture of me with Jack Straw was projected to the audience.

The screen went blank and I wiped my eyes as Carol introduced Chris Tarrant. He had been chosen to present the award because of his commitment to Sarah's Law, of which he was a vocal supporter. Stepping to the podium, Chris said, 'Of all the unforgettable people here today they really are a reason to make Britain very proud.'

As he finished, and the audience clapped, I wiped away a last tear before getting out of my seat and making my way to the front of the room, the images from the video cluttering my mind. I stepped up on to the stage and hugged Chris, as he presented me with the award. Half blinded by the bright lights, I looked out at the sea of faces and took a deep breath. 'Thanks very much.'

I could hear the quaver in my voice as I continued, 'I haven't seen those pictures for a long time. They've made me a bit tearful, I must say.'

Regaining a bit of my composure, I searched for my table and spoke directly to my mum. 'I wouldn't be standing here now if it wasn't for my family keeping me upright.' I then went on to thank our good friends, and ended the short speech with a promise: 'We will fight on, we will continue to fight until our children are safe on the streets. We are very proud to be British, very proud.'

It wasn't much, but it was all I could manage.

Chris took my arm and led me backstage, where he gave me a big heartfelt hug. 'If there is anything I can do to help with Sarah's Law, or to help you and Mike personally, I want you to let me know,' he said seriously.

He told me that he only lived a couple of miles from us in Surrey and we should call if we ever needed him. I thanked him, genuinely touched by his concern, and thought I might start to cry again.

To lighten the moment I joked, 'There is one thing you could do.'

'What's that?' he said.

'Well, I'd quite like to be a millionaire.'

He laughed. 'You'll have to work for that one, I'm afraid.'

The rest of the night passed by in a bit of a blur. After lunch there were drinks at the hotel bar. There was no VIP area for the celebrities, as that night it really was the award winners who were the stars, and everybody mingled comfortably together, uniting in the spirit of the occasion. Mum went round with her camera, snapping pictures, and I caught up with some members of the press who I'd got to know when Sarah was missing. The wine was free flowing and there was a general spirit of celebration in the air. I drank too much and, as I laughed and joked, thoughts of the fight the night before were temporarily wiped from my mind.

Later that evening Mum and I got a car home. On the way back the drink and emotion caught up with me and by the time I got back I was exhausted. As I walked in the house Mike and the children were sitting round watching television and eating a McDonalds.

'I'm sorry about last night,' he began.

I cut him off. 'I'm a bit drunk,' I said wearily, 'I won't remember any of this in the morning. Can we talk about it another time?'

Mike nodded. I kissed the children goodnight, and went upstairs to bed.

8

MIKE

After the disastrous Pride of Britain we should have learned our lesson and just stayed at home for the rest of that week. But we didn't, and in trying to put things right, we simply made them worse. The day after I came back from the awards, Mike and I made our peace and talked about trying to return to a more normal way of life.

'Why don't you go for a night out with the lads?' I suggested. 'You haven't been out like that for months.'

'I don't know,' said Mike, 'I wouldn't be very good company.'

'They're your friends, they don't care about that. Go on, it would do you good to do something normal, have a few pints, go to a club.'

'Maybe you're right,' he said, 'I don't want to go out round here though, I'll just get stared at all night.'

'Why don't you go up to the caravan?' I suggested.

It was a good idea. Sarah had never been to the caravan in Selsey, so it was free from the associations that were likely to bring Mike down. He called some friends down on the coast and they arranged to go out the very next night.

As Mike had been unable to drive the Savanna after Sarah's death, the *News of the World* had lent us an Audi A4 and it was this that he drove to Selsey to meet three friends. They were going out in Chichester and decided to drive there and pick up the car the next day. They had intended to go on a pub-crawl through town, but after the first few pubs and a game of pool they realised that Chichester nightlife midweek is a bit of a wash-out. After some discussion they decided to go and get some beers and head back to one of the lad's houses in Selsey to play cards. Mike was over the limit, but one of his friends insisted that he had only had two pints so he volunteered to drive to save them leaving the car.

It was a bad decision. The road was wet, he wasn't used to the car, and he was slightly over the limit. A few miles out of Chichester he lost control of the Audi on a roundabout and ended up in a ditch on the edge of a field, missing a lamp-post by inches. Luckily nobody was hurt and they climbed out of the car to assess the damage: there were some dents and scratches to the bodywork and it was stuck fast. It was late and they knew it would take ages to get a garage out to tow it, so they decided to leave the car where it was and come back in the morning. Mike was good with cars, especially bodywork, and he knew he'd be able to mend it himself.

The group started walking back towards Selsey, drinking the cans of lager they'd bought on the way. Then, a mile or so down the road, a police car pulled up. It turned out that another motorist had reported the accident and described Mike and his friends. When questioned about the incident Mike explained what had happened and said the car was his. But when the police did a registration check they found that the Audi wasn't registered to Mike, but to a company in London, and Mike didn't have any documentation to back up his story that it had been legitimately loaned to him by the newspaper.

The group were arrested and taken to the police station where Mike was breathalysed and found to be over the limit. He explained to officers that he hadn't been driving the car, but they didn't believe him, thinking his friend was covering up for him. They also didn't believe that the car had been loaned to him, even though they knew who Mike was and what he had been through. The matter should have been sorted out quickly and easily with a few phone calls, but for some reason the police kept him for hours, going over the same questions. Perhaps they were trying to prove the point that he didn't merit any special treatment.

In the early hours of the morning the phone woke me up. When a policeman introduced himself on the other end, my heart jumped. I knew that a call from the police at that hour couldn't be anything good. The officer explained what had happened and put Mike on the phone, who asked me to call the *News of the World* and get them to speak to the police. After hanging up, I rang Hayley Barlow and she called the police and verified that the car belonged to the company and had been loaned to us. The police finally let Mike go and he got a cab home.

The next day the trouble just continued, as the farmer whose field they had crashed into was threatening to sue for damages. It turned out that the car had knocked down part of his fence and some of his sheep had escaped. Hayley came down to help us sort it out, and she spent an afternoon helping the farmer herd up his wayward sheep and persuading him not to sue. Looking back on it now I can see the funny side, but at the time it felt like everything we did went wrong. Life was so unstable, we were only ever a minute away from a scene or fight of some kind. Many of the incidents could have been stopped before they started if we had only sat down and talked through how we were feeling. But we weren't that kind of family.

Like the Pride of Britain awards, we would start out with good and positive outlooks, but by the end of the day things would inevitably go to pot. The first anniversary of Sarah's death was another such occasion. The actual anniversary was on 1 July, which, a year on, was a Sunday. We expected things to be tough for us that day, but it was actually the day before, on the Saturday, that it hit us. We went to the pub with Jenny and Ian to take our minds off things, but it was impossible to forget. Every time I looked at my watch that day I would think of what we were doing at that time a year ago. At 5 p.m. I thought, 'We were in the car on the way down to Sussex now.' At 6 p.m. I thought, 'We were eating tea now.' At around the critical time I said to Mike, 'This time last year we were looking for Sarah.'

He turned to me and said, 'That's exactly what I was thinking. I've been thinking it all day, going through what was happening last year.'

'So have I,' I said softly, tears forming in my eyes.

Jenny and Ian noticed that we were getting emotional and suggested we go back to their house for a few drinks. We gratefully accepted, and that night we drank until we passed out.

The next day we all visited Sarah's grave. Mike, Charlotte and I went in the morning and were upset to see that it wasn't looking as pretty as it normally did. There had been a lot of rain, the grass was overgrown, dead flowers were scattered around, and there was still no headstone. Charlotte set to work, tidying away the dead flowers and weeds, chattering as she went. She wasn't exactly talking to Sarah, but she was speaking as if Sarah could hear her. We had taken a candle and a toy fairy with us and, after her grave was clean, we lit the candle and placed the fairy beside it. Later in the day Lee and Luke made their own visits to their sister's grave with their friends. They hadn't told their mates that it was the anniversary of Sarah's death, but both sets of friends remembered and simply turned up at the door with flowers. You wouldn't think teenage boys could be so thoughtful, but they had always looked on Sarah as their own sister and when she died it affected them deeply.

It had been an incredibly tense weekend. By late Sunday afternoon an argument was brewing between Mike and me and I knew there was going to be trouble. We were sitting watching television in the living room when Mike suddenly jumped up.

'I can't take this. I'm going.'

'What do you mean you're going? Where?'

'Anywhere. I can't stay here.'

'Mike, please don't go,' I pleaded.

'I have to. I can't just sit here like nothing's happened. I'm not like you, Sara.'

'What do you mean you're not like me? Are you saying I'm not hurting too?'

'Well, if you are, you never show it. It's like you've built a wall around your heart and nobody can get in. You always shut me out – how do you think that makes me feel?'

'We're different, Mike, that's all,' I tried to reason with him. 'Just because I don't go around in tears all the time doesn't mean I don't feel it.'

'If you just told me how you were feeling I could help.'

I looked at the floor. Seeing it was pointless, Mike snapped, 'I'm going to the caravan.'

And with that, he practically ran out of the house, slamming the front door behind him. I thought about going after him, but I knew there was no point. When he snapped I often tried to get him to calm down, but it usually only infuriated him further.

Mike did go to the caravan that night, and he stayed there for the next two days. I called him, and he assured me he was all right and just needed to be on his own for a while. I tried my best to understand, but I couldn't help worrying about him, hoping that his depression wasn't going to kick in too badly. I also felt sorry for myself, feeling rejected and alone. He later told me that he had spent the time drinking, crying, drinking more, and crying more. When he had got some of it out of his system he came home drained and we patched things up as best we could, until the next time.

At Mike's darkest moments he would dwell on exactly what he wanted to do to Roy Whiting. He usually tried to keep his thoughts from me, but at times, often when we had both been drinking, it would all come pouring out. He would go into the most horrendous detail, talking about torturing Whiting in the worst ways imaginable, taking him to the brink of death again and again before finishing him off. As I listened to him, part of me wondered how the man I loved could think about doing such terrible things to another human being, and I felt angry that Whiting could have made Mike into a person I didn't recognise. But there was another part of me – a big part – that thought it was OK for him to feel like that. Perhaps it was even healthy that he could express these emotions. I convinced myself that because he was able to vent his feelings he was probably less likely to actually act on them.

But I didn't realise how far down the line Mike had gone into turning his fantasies into reality. Hurting Whiting was more than just a dream for him. It was something he was determined to do and, during one of his dark, drunken moments, he told me exactly how.

'If he gets off, I'll do it, you know.'

'Don't say that, Mike.'

He looked me in the eye. 'I'm serious. I've got a shotgun.'

My blood ran cold. 'What? Where did you get a gun? Is it here in the house?'

'I got it from a bloke in the pub. Don't worry, it's not here, it's hidden somewhere safe. I've paid for it, I just need to collect it when I'm ready.'

I couldn't believe what I was hearing. 'How long have you had it?'

'Since last year, before he was charged. The police knew it was him, but they couldn't prove it. He was in prison for nicking a car, but I knew he wouldn't be in for long. He would have got away with it. And he would have done it again.'

'They would have been watching him.'

'They couldn't watch him all the time. If he wanted to do it again he'd find a way, you know that. I couldn't let him.'

I was reeling. If the police hadn't found the evidence to charge Whiting while he was still in prison, Mike would have shot him.

'They've got him now. Why haven't you got rid of it?'

'I'm not getting rid of it until he's found guilty. If he gets off he's dead.'

'Are you stupid?' I shouted. 'They'll lock you up. How do you think that would affect me and the kids?'

'I've worked it all out,' he said. 'I'll snatch him off the street like he did Sarah, drive him to the middle of nowhere, and shoot him in the head. Then I'll set fire to the car to get rid of the evidence. Nobody will connect me to him. I'll get away with it.'

'No, you won't,' I screamed. 'You'll be the first suspect the police will look at. And you'll go to prison – it's murder. How do you think the kids will feel when you're put away? Do you want them to think of their dad as a killer – no better than him?'

'How can you say that?' Mike shouted. 'It's because of him that I'm like this. He's made me this.'

Mike was right. Whiting had made Mike into this person filled with hatred, and I didn't know how to make it better.

I hate guns with a passion. I'd been terrified of them ever since Mike and I had been to a firing range on our first family holiday before Sarah was born. It was all done in controlled circumstances, with proper instructors and targets in some woodland, and we had gone for a bit of fun, to try something different. But as I held the gun in front of me and pulled the trigger, I was amazed by how the vibrations shook my whole body. I couldn't believe how powerful the gun was. You see actors on television waving them around like toys, and kids on the streets even carry them. But after that experience I couldn't even bear to see children playing with toy guns. I couldn't bear the thought of Mike with one.

Now that Mike had told me what he planned to do, I couldn't turn a blind eye and pretend it wasn't happening. If I did and he went through with it, I would have to live with that on my conscience. It wasn't that I thought Whiting deserved to live, but I didn't think it was our place to decide that. We had to put our trust in the justice system and let them deal with him. Also, if Mike did anything stupid he would end up in prison himself. I had lost my daughter and I wasn't prepared to lose my husband too. I knew that nothing I could say would make Mike change his mind, so I decided to take drastic action and go to the police.

When I told Martyn what Mike had revealed, he said to me, 'Sara, you can't tell me something like that and not expect me to deal with it.'

'I know,' I replied. 'That's why I'm telling you. I want you to do something about it before he does anything we'll all regret.'

So Martyn briefed Sean to have a chat with Mike, which he did, telling him that no matter what he had been through, he wasn't above the law.

'We will arrest you,' he warned Mike.

Although initially angry with me for going to the police, Mike understood why I had done it and eventually promised me that he wouldn't do anything stupid. Although I wanted to believe him, a niggling doubt played in the back of my mind and I knew that I would not be totally at ease until Whiting was behind bars for good. In this way, the trial couldn't come soon enough.

Yet, as much as I longed for Whiting's conviction, I was dreading what we would have to go through to get there. We had long since decided to attend every minute of the trial in November, meaning that we would be brought face to face with our daughter's killer on a daily basis. It might seem like we were torturing ourselves unnecessarily, but we felt we had to be there. Whiting had seemed totally remorseless so far, never showing a flicker of emotion. We thought that if he saw our faces staring at him every minute he was in that courtroom, it might bring home what he had done. There was also another reason. Sarah had no choice but to bear the most terrible experience, she could not walk away. Neither would we. The least we could do for her was listen to the details of her ordeal and face her killer.

As well as being emotionally harrowing, the trial was shaping up to be physically exhausting, as it was to take place at Lewes Crown Court in West Sussex, over 50 miles from our home in Surrey. Terry and Les said that we were welcome to stay with them for the duration of the trial, as they would also be attending every day, but we decided against it. We wanted there to be a minimum of disruption for the children, who had asked if they could keep going to school during the trial, so we decided to stay in Surrey and travel to and from court every day. Dave and Sean offered to take it in turns to pick us up in the morning and take us back after court finished in the afternoon, and between my mum, Fiona and Jenny, the children would be well cared for.

The upcoming trial also brought the issue of the press back into sharp focus, as they had all been back in touch, trying to secure interviews for after the trial. Mike had long since made his feelings clear on the issue of the media, and he didn't want to do any interviews at all post-trial. I agreed that we would not feel like doing rounds and rounds of interviews, as we would be drained, but thought that we should at least do some. For me, it was a way of keeping Sarah's Law in the public eye. After long discussions we reached a compromise: we would do one exclusive interview with the *News of the World*, as they had started the Sarah's Law campaign and were still battling for changes. We would also do a five-minute press conference on the steps of the court after the verdict to be fair to other media. Mike agreed that he would be involved, with one proviso: this would be the last interview he ever did. I agreed.

9

THE TRIAL

When we arrived in Lewes on the morning of Tuesday, 13 November, it was pandemonium. The high street had been taken over by police, camera crews, reporters and members of the public. The hotel opposite the court, the White Hart, had been booked solid by the press and there were photographers hanging out of every window. When we were dropped off outside the courtroom there were calls for us to pose for pictures and we dutifully stopped on the steps while cameras flashed around us. For once we had forsaken our jeans and T-shirts and were smartly dressed, me in a grey pinstriped suit and Mike in black.

We were both dying for a smoke before going into court, but we didn't want to linger outside longer than we had to, so we decided on caffeine as a substitute and headed for the canteen. The place was packed, but a couple of reporters we recognised stood up and offered us their seats. We exchanged pleasantries with them but they did not try to engage us in conversation about the trial, for which we were grateful. As we sipped our hot drinks, Dave pointed out a couple to us, sitting in a corner, looking bleak.

'Do you know who they are?' he said.

'I don't think so,' I replied. 'Should I?'

'They're the parents of Whiting's other victim, the little girl from Crawley.'

I studied them and nodded slowly. Looking at the husband was like looking at Mike. He was such a big man, and his grief and anger were written all over his face, in the set of his mouth and jaw, the dark circles under his eyes. I could understand them wanting to be there. They needed to make sure that Whiting was locked away for good this time – as he should have been after attacking their daughter. The girl, now in her teens, was to be spared giving evidence against Whiting, as the judge had decided in pre-trial argument not to allow details of the previous conviction to be admissible. Initially we were dismayed by the ruling, but the police explained to us that it might be a blessing in disguise. If the evidence was used, and a conviction was obtained on the basis of it, Whiting could later argue that he hadn't been given a fair trial, paving the way for a potentially successful appeal.

After a coffee we headed upstairs to the family room we had been assigned for the duration of the case. Crammed into the little box room were our parents, brothers, sisters and cousins, chattering away nervously, looking uncomfortable in clothes usually reserved for best. As we walked in we were engulfed by hugs and words of support and we felt lucky to have such a big supportive family. Within no time a clerk appeared and told us all to make our way into the courtroom – everybody, that is, except me. I was first witness for the Crown, which meant that I was not allowed to enter the court before I gave my evidence. It had also meant that I had not been allowed to talk about the case in any detail to anyone. The same went for Lee, who was to give evidence via video link. It had been hard, but we had been very strict with ourselves about keeping to the rules, as we didn't want anything to jeopardise the trial.

It was hard having to stay behind as the family filed out, but there was nothing we could do about it. Finally there was just me and Mike left in the room. Giving me a hug, he asked, 'Do you want me to stay here with you?'

It was a nice idea, but I shook my head. 'I'll be fine. I want him to know that at least one of us is there.'

He nodded his understanding, kissed the top of my head, and left.

It was a long day for me, sitting in that little room reading papers, or smoking cigarettes on the court steps. But members of the family popped in and out of court to let me know how things were going and to give me some support. In the middle of the afternoon, Les came to see me. She looked worried.

'What's up?' I asked.

'It could be something or nothing,' she said hesitantly, 'I don't know.'

'Go on,' I urged her.

'It's just that when the jury were sworn in earlier there was something nagging at me and I wasn't sure what. Now I've got it. I've met one of the jurors.'

'Who is it?'

'She's the girlfriend of someone at work. I don't know her well, but I've met her. What shall I do?'

There was no question in my mind. 'We've got to tell someone. We've got to do everything by the book, we can't take any chances.'

'Oh, I feel terrible!' Les said. 'We'll have to start over again.'

'It's only been a day, it doesn't matter in the long run.'

'I suppose you're right,' Les sighed.

When the news reached the judge he ordered that the trial should be stopped and a new jury sworn in. There was no other option. Although there was only a tenuous link, it could be argued that the juror would not be impartial. So the trial started again the next day. It was 14 November, Mike's birthday, and needless to say we did nothing to celebrate the occasion. The rest of the week was taken up with opening speeches, and it soon became clear that I was not going to be called until the following week. Unable to stand being cooped up in that little room all day, I started going to a nearby pub where I could have a drink and a cigarette and talk on my mobile phone. Sometimes a member of the family or a police officer would join me, having a break from court, and at lunchtime everyone would pile in for sandwiches and to discuss how the case was going. The press quickly realised that this was where we all met, and respectfully left us alone, choosing to drink in another pub so we could have some privacy.

On Monday I was finally called to the stand. That morning I had dressed carefully in my long grey coat, pinstriped trousers and white blouse, and I was determined to hold my head up high and not allow Whiting to intimidate me. But as I walked into the courtroom for the first time, and saw him slouching in the dock wearing a dirty sweatshirt, jeans and a sneer, my legs almost buckled. I hesitated for a split second, then took a deep breath and put one foot in front of the other, doing what I needed to do. As I stepped up to the stand and was sworn in, Whiting was only a few feet away and I looked directly at him. The fact that he was too cowardly to even meet my eye gave me strength. I was the powerful one now, not him: he was nothing. My gaze then flickered past him to an older woman, dressed smartly in a blue coat and matching hat. She had been pointed out to me earlier. It was Whiting's mum, Pamela Green, and this was her first day at the trial. My heart went out to her. How must she feel, knowing that she had produced this monster?

The barrister for the Crown, Timothy Langdale, gently took me through the events of 1 July. I had been told to try and project my voice so the whole court could hear, but when I began talking it was in a soft, quiet voice. Somehow it didn't seem an appropriate story to shout out. I described how the family had travelled down to the coast to see Terry and Les, sat down to a meal of shepherd's pie, and then gone for a walk on the beach. As I got to the point where we left the children I took a deep breath and told the court, 'My last words to them were that they should stay together. As we were walking away, I looked back and there they were, playing on the beach.'

I carried on, telling how we went to see Terry's friend's house, stopped at the pub and the off-licence, and then made our way home, to find Les standing outside with Charlotte. At this point, my throat constricted and I found that my words had dried up. I simply could not bring myself to say that Sarah had gone. If I did, I might start to cry and I didn't want him to see my weakness. I looked at the ground before me and Timothy Langdale gave me a few seconds before gently asking if Sarah was missing. It was all I could do to nod my head.

After taking a few moments to compose myself, I finished telling the events of that day, before being asked to describe Sarah. I closed my eyes for a split second, saw my daughter in my mind, and again I had to look at the floor.

'She didn't have very long hair and had it in a short bob, about shoulder-length. It was possible she had a hairband around her wrist. She was wearing a deep-blue Fred Perry-type sports dress. It was very comfortable to put on for her. Sarah was quite small for her age. Her hair was blonde, going darker as she got older.'

As I stood lost in thought about Sarah's hair – dark as a baby, then blonde, then growing darker again as she grew up – I was brought down to earth by another question. Could I identify some exhibits for the court? A clerk brought over an evidence bag, inside of which was a blue sweatshirt, with the words Bell Farm stitched on the breast. I stroked the material through the plastic, identifying it for the court as Sarah's school sweatshirt. Next I was handed a silver quilted jacket. I smiled as I handled it. Terry and Les had given it to Sarah the previous Christmas and she adored it. The jacket had detachable arms and made her feel so grown-up that I could hardly get her to take it off. It had even come to Sussex with us that fateful day, despite the fact that it was the middle of summer. Like Sarah's other things, it had been taken away for forensic testing when she had been abducted, so it was the first time I had seen it in eighteen months. I was then handed a photograph of Sarah's shoe and I actually laughed as I identified it, telling the jury how hard Sarah had been on her shoes.

My evidence took just under twenty-five minutes and as it had been in the form of an agreed statement, it meant that I didn't have to be cross-examined, which was a great relief. It's not that I had anything to hide, I was simply scared of the line of questioning the defence might take. If they had tried to imply that I was an unfit mother for having left the children alone and gone to the pub, I don't think I could have taken it. I had beaten myself up about it enough, without other people doing it too. And why should I be the one to feel guilty when the man who had killed Sarah was sitting in front of me?

Throughout my testimony, Whiting had energetically scribbled notes on his A4 pad, and I wondered what he could possibly be writing. He had glanced up at me twice, but was careful never to meet my eye or show any emotion, and even when I left the stand he didn't look up. I walked towards the exit of the courtroom and was about to walk out, when something made me stop and turn round. I gave Whiting a long, hard stare in the dock, willing him to meet my eyes, but he steadfastly refused. Mike, who had seen what I was doing, was up and out of his chair in a flash. As he reached me I abruptly opened the door and we both left the courtroom, falling into each other's arms. I finally let go of the tears I had kept back during the past half-hour and sobbed on Mike's shoulder.

The last thing I wanted to do at that moment was go back into court, but it was Lee's evidence next and I had to be there. So I steeled myself again, and took a seat next to Mike to the side of the dock. We had known from the beginning that Lee would be a key witness and there had been lots of negotiations about how his testimony would be given, considering his age. The first suggestion was that he would give evidence in court, a curtain shielding him from the majority of the courtroom, including Whiting. To prepare him for this, Lee's court liaison officer, who visited weekly, took him to Lewes Crown Court to familiarise him with the setting. He sat him in the courtroom and put the judge's wig on his head. But Lee was unhappy with the idea of being in court. The thought of his sister's killer – whom he had already come face to face with once – being so close by was too hard to bear. The other option to be considered was a video link from another room of the court, but in the end an even better solution was found. If Lee was testifying via video link there was no real reason for him to be in the court building at all, so a neutral venue was arranged.

Now, television screens around the courtroom flickered to life. Before Lee's evidence began, taped police interviews with both brothers from the day after Sarah was abducted were to be shown to the court. I had not been present during the interviews, so when Luke's anxious face appeared on the screen my heart went out to him. For the next hour I watched as my youngest son was questioned by Detective Constable Sue Gunnis about what had happened in the field that day. She was as kind to him as she could be, but there were still times when he looked almost too distraught to carry on. He described how they had all been playing, before Sarah banged her head and ran off. Luke gave chase, before Charlotte was stung and he went back to tend to her. As he said, 'I was ten seconds away, ten seconds away from catching up with her,' I could tell that he was on the verge of tears.

Luke then told how his brother had later mentioned that he had seen a man driving a white van in the lane. Looking down at his baseball boots and speaking quietly, he said, 'We thought it was a man out to get children, and then we got worried.' But by far the worst part of the interview came right at the end, when Luke was asked if he had any questions. I watched as my son jumped to his feet and blurted out, 'When do you reckon we'll get Sarah back?' There was a pause before the detective replied, 'I can't tell you that, but we are doing what we can.' Luke may have bravely held the tears back then, but I couldn't.

After a break, Lee's taped interview was played and he told how he had run into Peak Lane to find his sister. Sarah was nowhere to be seen, but there was a white van with a male driver. In describing him, Lee said:

'He looked scruffy. He looked like he had not shaved for ages. He had little white bristles on his face and there were little bits of grey in his hair which was greasy. His face was dirty and he had yellowish teeth when he grinned. His eyes were really white and stood out in his face. He looked like he had been through some bushes. He had on a red checked shirt. It also had black in it. He also had on a white shirt with the checked shirt over it.'

As Lee described Whiting, I felt so proud. He had only seen him for a few moments, yet his recall was crystal clear. The photofit he had provided police with was so accurate that officers commented that even as trained observers they couldn't have done a better job. Lee then told the courtroom how Whiting 'just sat there and grinned and waved at me and then went off. He smiled.' I looked up and saw the faces around me pale and the reporters' pens move swiftly across their pads. This bit of evidence showed Whiting as the monster he really was, snatching a little girl and then gloating to her brother.

When the interview drew to a close, it was time for Lee to be cross-examined via video link. As he appeared on screen my heart gave a lurch. He looked so small and vulnerable that I just wanted to tell everybody to turn off the television and leave my boy alone. I felt so protective towards him that I could hardly bear it. Whiting had already put one of my children through hell, and now here he was doing it to another. In those moments I didn't care about the trial or a conviction, I just wanted to shout, 'Stop!' But of course I couldn't, and to be fair to the defence barrister, Sally O'Neill, she was as respectful and considerate as possible. She gently questioned Lee about how far he was from the van in Peak Lane, the implication being that he could not have got a good look at Whiting's face. But although his voice shook as he clarified his evidence, Lee held his own, insisting that the van was just a few feet away and he had seen the driver clearly.

When I got home that night I gave Lee a huge hug and told him how proud I was of him. He shrugged it off, as teenage boys do, but I could tell that his mood had lightened. He was obviously very relieved to have got the ordeal over with. That night, like every other night of the trial, we tried to be as normal as we could. We got a take-away in, watched television, and asked the children about their days at school. Later, when they had gone to bed, Mike went to the pub and I stayed at home, relishing the time alone. I picked up *Harry Potter and the Chamber of Secrets* and started to read. During the course of the trial I read all the Harry Potter books. They transported me into a different world, a world where children were happy and laughing, and the evil force that threatens them is always defeated in the end. It made me sad that Sarah had died too young to have the pleasure of the books, as she would have loved the magical creatures, potions, spells and adventures. I pictured myself reading them to her at bedtime and her begging me for one more chapter.

It was happy thoughts of Sarah that got me through that time. As I sat in court listening to the details of my daughter's death, I would drift off into my own little world, thinking of happier times, or of her spirit, now free from suffering. During the long hours of forensic evidence from expert witnesses, which made up most of the case for the prosecution, I would sit and daydream about Sarah. Sometimes I even became convinced that Sarah's spirit was there in the court with us, playing mischievous tricks. There was a door behind where Whiting sat in the dock that led to the cells below, and as I looked at it one day I imagined it opening and him tipping backwards and falling down the stairs. I couldn't believe it when the door actually opened slightly as I stared at it, and I smiled, convinced that it was Sarah trying to get her own back on him. I could see her cheeky face in my mind and hear her saying, 'Come on, Mummy, let's make him fall down the stairs and hurt himself, that will teach him.' A minute later the prison officer in the dock noticed the door ajar and reached over to close it. Seconds later it had popped open again. The same ritual was performed six or seven times and I had to put my hand over my mouth to stop myself giggling along with Sarah.

If anyone had seen me they would have thought I was mad, smiling at such a time, but I needed these times of light relief, for sometimes there was no escaping the horror. While I could tune out evidence about fibres or strands of hair, there was no blocking out some of the forensic evidence. All along the police had tried to be tactful and considerate with us when dealing with the more gruesome aspects of Sarah's death, being careful never to reduce her to 'a body' or a 'victim'. To them she was always Sarah, our little girl. But the courtroom was different, as the doctors and scientists had to present their evidence in a totally dispassionate, objective way, and it could make for very difficult listening.

On Wednesday, 21 November, it all got too much for us, as pathologist Vesna Djurovic, who had performed Sarah's post-mortem, gave her evidence. We had been told to prepare ourselves for the worst, and Mike and I huddled together protectively as she began. In a matter-of-fact voice she told the court that our daughter had met a 'violent' death, 'probably asphyxia', in a 'sexually motivated homicide'. Continuing, she said it was impossible to say what injuries Sarah had suffered, as her body was very decomposed and had been attacked by animals. My heart was thumping hard and Mike was shaking beside me as she went a stage further, saying that as Sarah's body had been removed from the ground her hair had remained attached to the underlying soil. It was too much for Mike, who jumped abruptly out of his seat and ran for the door.

I couldn't blame him for leaving, but I was determined to stay. My brother Paul immediately came and took Mike's place, putting his arm around me, as I steeled myself against the pathologist's words. I flinched as she said that Sarah's four-foot, 'well nourished' body was discovered naked with dry vegetation attached to it. It was, she continued, in a 'moderately advanced state of decomposition and mummification'. That did it for me, my determination was lost, and I too fled the courtroom. That was our princess they were talking about, not some biological specimen. I found Mike in the pub, looking white. I sat down with him, ordered a pint and lit up.

'Have they finished?' he asked.

'No, but I couldn't take any more,' I replied. 'I know we said we wanted to be there every minute of the trial, but I can't sit through that.'

'Nor me. When she started talking about Sarah's hair I couldn't stand it. I kept thinking about how proud she was of her long blonde hair when she was little and how she liked brushing it. I thought I'd go for Whiting if I stayed.'

So we made an agreement there and then not to put ourselves through that again. We would continue going to the trial every day and start each morning in the courtroom, but if the evidence showed signs of being particularly gruelling we would leave. There was no shame in that.

I returned to court later, but Mike couldn't face it, and when the judge adjourned the case for the day there was still no sign of him. Finally, my brother went out to search for Mike and found him in another pub, drunk. Paul told him that Dave was ready to take us home, but Mike refused to budge. There was no point arguing, it would only spark a row, so we decided that I should go back to Surrey and Mike should stay with Paul in Sussex. They drank until closing time and later went back to Paul's house, where he looked after Mike, letting him shout and rant and rave. Paul was such a big, strong bloke that Mike could take out all his frustrations on him without fear of doing any physical harm.

When the case for the prosecution drew to a close I was completely satisfied. I had never doubted that Whiting had done it and, after hearing all the evidence, I was sure the jury would be convinced too. There was simply too much forensic evidence linking Whiting to Sarah to be ignored. Everybody was waiting for the defence to begin with great anticipation, as it had been confirmed that Whiting was going in the box. Funny as it sounds, I was looking forward to it. He had never given a full account of that day, simply repeating 'no comment' in police interviews, and I wanted to see what he had to say for himself. I also wanted to see if he would remain as emotionless as he had so far. Surely when faced with direct questions about killing Sarah, with me and Mike sitting there, he would crack? I was desperate for him to show some sign that he knew what he had done was wrong.

On Tuesday, 4 December, queues for the public gallery were even longer than usual. As we waited for people to take their seats, one of the prison officers standing in the dock turned and looked me in the eye. 'You all right, love?' he asked kindly. I gave him a smile and nodded my head. Then he reached into his pocket and brought out a packet of mints. 'Polo?' he asked, and I took one, thanking him. He then proceeded to offer the packet round the whole family. It was a small gesture, but somehow it meant a lot at the time. It may have been his job to guard and protect Whiting, but he was telling us that he was on our side. Then the familiar words, 'All rise!' were shouted out, and court began.

Holding Mike's hand, I stared straight at Whiting as he was led to the witness box. He hadn't even bothered to smarten himself up for his big day, dressed in his usual jeans and a dark red sweatshirt. Up to that point I had yet to hear him speak properly and when he started to give his account of 1 July 2000 his voice grated immediately. He had a missing front tooth so dropped his Rs sometimes, making him difficult to understand. Slouching in the dock, looking relaxed, he claimed that he had been 'bored and fed up' that day and wanted time alone to think. He said that he had visited three parks, a boating lake and a funfair, and gone for a walk on the beach on the Sussex coast. He didn't say it, but everybody in the court knew: he hadn't gone to these places to think, but to look for a child to abduct.

As he came to the end of his account, Sally O'Neill cut to the chase. 'You are charged with the kidnap and murder of Sarah Payne. Have you in any shape or form been associated with that young girl?'

He didn't even hesitate. 'No.'

'Or had anything to do with her death?' she pressed.

Again the glib lie. 'Nothing whatsoever.'

'You know that you do not need to give evidence in this case – why have you given evidence?'

'I want the jury to hear what I have to say. I've got nothing to hide and I've told the truth.'

I shook my head and Mike whispered, 'Lying bastard.' It was a pathetic display.

One of the newspapers commented the next day that Timothy Langdale cross-examined Whiting like a 'Rottweiler' – and they were spot on. Skipping the niceties, he went right for the jugular and had accused Whiting of Sarah's murder within two minutes. He began by asking why, if he was innocent, he had not just given the police a full and frank account of his actions that day.

Whiting replied, 'I don't know. Possibly they wouldn't have believed me.'

Timothy Langdale challenged him, 'The reason is, you were having a bit of difficulty trying to tell the police where you had been the previous evening.'

'No.'

'Because you had, in fact, been involved in the kidnap of this very little girl they had come to you to talk about. True?'

'Not true.'

'That was the problem, wasn't it?'

'No.'

'You were trying to conceal from the police not only what you were doing on the Saturday, but also on the Sunday. That's where you were having trouble. You had not worked out your story.'

'I had no story to work out.'

'The reason you were not telling them the truth as an innocent man was that you were a guilty man.'

'That's not true.'

When quizzed about the evidence, Whiting claimed that a series of coincidences led him to be there. It was coincidence that he drove a white van like the one Lee had seen; coincidence that he owned similar clothes to the ones Lee described; coincidence that he too had a gap in his teeth; coincidence that he had cleaned his van and changed its doors the weekend of Sarah's abduction; coincidence that he had baby oil, a knife, cable ties and a spade in the back of his van; coincidence that fibres from his sweatshirt were found on Sarah's shoe and fibres from his socks found in her hair.

'So it's a whole series of unfortunate coincidences?' asked Timothy Langdale incredulously, and Whiting agreed. The defence really had no case.

On the nineteenth day of the trial, when the jury were sent out to consider their verdict, Lee and Luke came to court with us. It had been a battle to get them there, but it was one we had eventually won. Technically they were too young to be in the courtroom, but after what they had been through we thought this was ridiculous. They had been involved in the case right from the start, being questioned and filmed by police for hours, attending identity parades, and ultimately giving evidence. And they had done it all with a maturity far greater than their years. The only thing they had asked for in return was to be in court to see the man who killed their sister imprisoned. How could we deny them that? In the end, the matter was taken all the way to the judge who decided that he would make an exception in this case and the boys would be allowed in court.

When the jury was sent out I thought that they would be back within an hour or so with a guilty verdict. But, as I sat with the family in the court canteen, an hour stretched into two, and before we knew it the judge was dismissing the jury for the night, to continue again the next day.

'Why are they taking so long?' I asked Sean. 'Is it a bad sign?'

'Well, generally speaking, the longer a jury are out, the more likely it is they'll come back with a not guilty . . .'

He must have seen my face pale, as he quickly continued, 'But in big, high-profile cases like this, where there is a lot of evidence to consider, it's more likely that they're just being thorough. I don't think we have to start worrying yet.'

On the way home I thought about what Sean had said. I had never really considered before what a hard job the jury had. They had a man's life in their hands and they had to treat that responsibility very seriously, going over the evidence with a fine-tooth comb to ensure there was no room for doubt.

On the second day of deliberations, we stayed in the court building at first, wanting to be nearby for when the verdict came in. But as the hours went by we couldn't bear it any longer. We could have taken the boys and gone for a walk, but we needed a drink so we guiltily left them with the family and went to the pub, where we sat drinking, smoking and waiting for the phone to ring. It felt like those seventeen days when we waited for news of Sarah, every minute stretching out into an hour. The longer the jury were out, the more anxious we got. We wanted them to be thorough, but surely they had had plenty of time to go through the evidence? What was holding them up? The thought of a not guilty verdict, or even a retrial, was unbearable.

Finally, on the third day, the call came as we were sitting in the pub in the early afternoon: after eight hours and forty minutes the jury had reached a verdict. The whole family was there that day and, as we hurried down the road back to the courthouse, we looked like a gang. As we took our seats for the last time, Mike and Terry were flanked by police officers to stop them doing anything stupid. The boys were sitting separately from us, with their social worker and two police officers, by the doors, in case they needed to get out quickly. We thought that the jury would come in straight away, but we were faced with more waiting and, as the minutes ticked on, Mike got increasingly agitated. After half an hour of sitting there he jumped up and dashed out of the court. I didn't want to go after him, as I was afraid I would miss the jury coming back, so Martyn went to find him.

'Try to be calm,' I said when he got back.

'Why should I?' he said angrily. 'Why should I be calm at a time like this? If I can't be wound up now, when can I?'

Finally the jury filed in, followed by the judge, and the courtroom went silent. The tension around us was incredible. This was it, the moment we had been waiting for, for one year and 193 days. The foreman of the jury was asked to stand up, and a young woman rose out of her seat. The judge asked her if the jury had reached a verdict and she said they had. I gripped Mike's hand tightly and the whole court seemed to hold its breath as he asked how they found the defendant on the count of kidnap. The foreman looked at Whiting, then at Mike and me, and back at Mike, and she said in a clear, strong voice: 'Guilty.'

Around us, the family hissed 'yesssss', but Mike and I just sat holding each other, our breath drawn in, heads down, waiting for the next verdict – that of murder. As the foreman was again asked for her verdict, all I could think of was Sarah. My daughter's face, her giggle, her smile. Then came the words we had been waiting to hear, as the foreman practically shouted out: 'Guilty!' I hadn't realised how much tension I had been holding inside up until that moment. As I let out my breath, my whole body felt like a balloon that had been deflated, and I started to sob with relief. Beside me I was aware of Mike shouting out 'YES!' and then collapsing in sobs in my arms.

As a family we hold our feelings in a lot, putting on a brave face for the world, but at that moment none of us held anything in. For once we let down our guard and did whatever came naturally. As Mike and I cried, the family around us clapped, cheered, sobbed and hugged one another. The judge indulged us for a few minutes, before bringing the courtroom back to order. Then Timothy Langdale rose from his seat. Finally, he was able to tell the court about Whiting's previous conviction, telling how he had snatched another little girl off the street, threatened and sexually assaulted her.

As his words sank in, members of the jury started to cry, appalled at Whiting's crime, and also relieved that they had come to the right verdict. I looked across to where the little girl's parents were sitting. Her mum was crying and clutching her husband's arm, almost as if she were holding him back. Then, all of a sudden, I remembered that the boys were in court, listening to what the petrified girl had endured. Inevitably they would be seeing their sister going through the same thing in their minds. I had to hold them. Stumbling out of my seat I tried to reach my sons, but the court was so packed that I couldn't get through and I finally gave up, holding on to a pillar for support.

After Timothy Langdale sat down, the judge began to speak. Looking straight at Whiting, he said, 'You are indeed an evil man. You are in no way mentally unwell. I have seen you for a month and, in my view, you are a glib and cunning liar.

'I have a psychiatrist's report which assists me, and a psychiatrist who saw you in June 1995 said you were a high-risk repeat offender. How right he was.

'My judgment is that you are, and will remain, an absolute menace to any little girl. This is one of the rare cases when I shall recommend to the appropriate authorities that you will be kept in prison for the rest of your life.'

At these words I began sobbing again, as the court exploded into cheers, claps and shouts. Even the police officers joined in. We had done it. Whiting would never be able to harm another little girl again.

The judge called for order, and continued, 'You are every parent's and every grandparent's nightmare come true. It is important that children are allowed to have some freedom by their parents and others to learn self-reliance and enjoy their childhood. You exploited this for your own abnormal sexual desires.'

As the judge delivered his damning words, Whiting merely stood there, arms folded, staring straight ahead with no expression on his face. It was as if it had not happened to him. Even when the judge uttered the words, 'Take him down', and Terry leaned over the dock and shouted, 'I hope you rot!', he still did not blink an eye.

10

AFTERMATH

At the end of the trial my first instinct was to go to Sarah's grave. I needed to tell my little girl that the bad man who had taken her away from us had been put away and could never harm another child. It wasn't much to ask, but sadly I was denied this as, by coincidence, the last day of the trial was also the day that Sarah's headstone was finally completed and placed at her grave. When the press found out that the stone had been put up, they saw a photo opportunity and we were told that they were lying in wait for us to visit after Whiting's conviction. It was an agonising decision, but in the end we decided not to go. Telling Sarah what had happened was a private affair and we didn't want long-lens cameras pointing at us from the bushes. We also got our solicitor to put out a request for pictures of Sarah's headstone not to be printed. We couldn't bear seeing it in the newspapers before we had seen it ourselves.

Although most of the papers respected our wishes, I was devastated to find that a couple did not. As I opened one of the papers on Saturday I was horrified to see Sarah's headstone staring back at me, and I quickly shut the paper as tears sprang to my eyes. We had given the press so much, never refusing interviews without a good reason, and we had never asked them for anything in return. I remembered Mike Alderson's words months before, warning us that if we went exclusive other sections of the press might turn against us. I had convinced myself that they wouldn't, but perhaps he had been right: we were paying the price for signing exclusively to the *News of the World* after the trial. I knew that until our interviews were printed on Sunday there would still be papers out there looking for stories.

It was the first real occasion that we had not been in control of the press, and we felt betrayed. Some of the papers also called for a return of the death penalty in Sarah's name, which upset me. Years before, when I first became a mum, I remember sitting around with friends discussing capital punishment. I was vehemently against it as I don't believe that a civilised society can condone killing in any form. One of my friends said to me at the time, 'What if one of your children was murdered?' but I insisted that I would not want their killer to be given the death penalty. Never in a million years did I think my convictions would be tested, but it was a view I had stuck to.

After a terrible five-day wait, we finally went to the graveyard on Sunday afternoon. After checking that all the photographers had gone, we walked over to Sarah's grave with its brand-new marble headstone. Under a picture of Sarah in her blue Bell Farm sweatshirt were the words:

SARAH EVELYN ISOBEL
PAYNE
Aged 8
Born 13th October 1991
Taken from us on 1st July 2000

She took a lighted candle
Into a room we cannot find,
But we know she was here,
Because the happiness she left behind.

Rest in Peace little Princess
Forever missed our beautiful Daughter and Sister

She'll never really leave us.
She will live on in us all
The way she Cared, Shared
And made us Happy.

Grand daughter, cousin, niece
& Friend.

It was beautiful. We just wished that the whole world had not seen it before us. As Charlotte performed her usual ritual of tidying her older sister's grave, Mike placed fresh flowers on it, and the boys stood there silently, I knelt by Sarah's grave and started speaking to her softly. 'You're safe now, princess,' I told her. 'He can't hurt you or anyone else any more. He's been put in prison for ever. You really can rest in peace now. There's nothing more to fear. I love you.'

As I uttered the words, I realised that they applied as much to me as they did to Sarah. People kept talking about 'closure', telling me that once Whiting had been jailed the family would be able to 'move on with our lives' and 'put it behind us'. And it was true that with him in prison for life, many of our fears had been taken away. There was no question of him re-offending. No fear of Mike seeking revenge. No worries about him coming after our other children. Perhaps this would be the 'full stop' we had been waiting for. Maybe it spelt a new chapter in our lives and we could finally get back to normal.

The children were going to school regularly again and Mike was working, but I still could not face going back to work. I told myself that I just wasn't ready and would start looking for a job the next week or next month. Knowing that I was facing a lot of time on my own, I planned to get the house in order and finally make it a home. When we moved into Riverside Road just before Sarah's funeral we had literally put the crates in the garage, unzipped our suitcases, and just got on with it. Over a year on, our meagre possessions still spilled out of boxes, used and then discarded on the floor. There were no little touches that made it homely, no ornaments or plants on the mantelpiece, no paintings by the children on the fridge. The only thing to personalise the front room was a smiling portrait of Sarah in her school uniform over the sofa. Now, with nothing else on my mind, I could finally unpack our things properly and make our house a nice place to be. I could cook the children tea when they got in and make sure they had clean clothes to wear. I could be a mum again.

The Monday after the trial ended I got up early and made the children breakfast, before walking Charlotte to school. I was going to get something in for tea on the way home, but as I walked into the shop I saw my grief-stricken face staring back at me from one of the front pages. I walked straight out and, telling myself I'd pop out later, I went home. Walking into the front room, I swept newspapers and coats off the sofa on to the floor, and sat down, switching on the television. *Kilroy* was on, so I lay on the sofa and watched the show, temporarily distracted by other people's problems and lives. I only meant to watch for an hour, but before I knew it, it was lunchtime. Although I wasn't hungry I knew I should eat so I opened the fridge. There was some milk, butter and hard cheese, but that was about it. I put some bread in the toaster and ate two pieces of toast and jam standing at the kitchen work-top, before wandering back into the living room and sitting down in front of the television again until it was time to fetch Charlotte. I'd go shopping tomorrow. We could have McDonalds tonight.

Tomorrow came and went and there was still no food in the fridge or tea on the table. I used to do the bare minimum to keep the household going: doing the laundry when we had no clean clothes left, cooking dinner, tidying up. But what little I had done around the house had now dwindled into nothing. It was as much as I could do to drag myself out of bed in the mornings and take Charlotte to school. After I had done this, I would go straight home and lie on the sofa watching daytime telly. I barely even registered what I was watching, it was just something to fill the silence and take me away from my life. I didn't eat or even have a cup of tea, as I simply couldn't be bothered to make anything. Sometimes Jenny would come over and we would sit around chatting, which helped. I would be fine when she was there, but as soon as she left to go to work I would sink back into apathy.

Sitting at home alone, I never cried; there was just a deadness, a nothingness. I was simply existing. It seemed that the less I did, the less I was able to do, and gradually I found it more and more difficult to leave the house at all. I would make excuses why I couldn't go out, or say to myself that I would go in an hour or after the next chat show. But the journey was always put off. Most days, picking Charlotte up from school was the only thing I absolutely had to do, so it was the only thing I did.

When I returned home with her, I would wake Mike – who was still working nights and sleeping days – at 4 p.m.

'Have I got a clean T-shirt?' he might ask.

'Look in the drawer.'

'I have, there's none there. Didn't you put any laundry in the machine?'

'No.'

'Why not?'

'Didn't get round to it.'

Going downstairs, he would open the fridge, looking for something to eat before work.

'Didn't you go to the shops?'

'No.'

'What have you been doing all day?'

I would shrug. 'Pick something up on your way to work.'

'Well, I'll have to, won't I?' he would say, before going to work, stomach empty.

Mike wasn't the kind of man to expect a spotless house, and had always been happy to live in a casual, sloppy way. But this, he argued, was getting ridiculous. At the time I felt that he was being unreasonable. After what had happened, everything else seemed so trivial. Our daughter was dead: what did it matter if there were no clean clothes or dinner on the table?

Over the eighteen months since Sarah's death, our home life had completely changed. At Arch Road the house had always been full, busy and happy. The children's friends dropped around almost every day after school to play or stay for tea. They often spent almost as much time with Mike and me as the children, as we all sat around laughing and joking like one big happy family. Now, since Sarah's death, the spirit of fun had gone from the house. Luke seemed most affected by the atmosphere and he started spending all his time away from home. He would come in from school, dump his bags, and be straight out the door again, returning ten minutes before his curfew time. He didn't want to be with us any more, and who could blame him? Lee still brought friends home, and when they were there I tried to make the effort to have a laugh with them like I used to, but everyone could tell my heart wasn't in it. It was like I was a shell of my previous self – there, but not.

On those evenings when the house was empty, I started drinking by myself, something I had never done before. Drinking had always been a social thing for Mike and me, and later, after Sarah's death, something we did together to dull the pain. Now I poured myself glass after glass of wine as I sat in front of the telly, until I fell into bed, drunk and exhausted. Although I woke every morning with a hangover, I still didn't stop. I was so low that I didn't even realise there was anything wrong with my behaviour.

As the weeks and months wore on, Mike started to get increasingly frustrated with me. He went to work every day, no matter how he felt, as he knew he had to bring in money to support us and, in going out to work, he had to deal with the pressures of the outside world, which I didn't. When we were in the news, Mike had to face people looking at him on the streets, but as I was practically a recluse by this time, I didn't have to handle any of that. I could shut the door and not see anyone, and I frequently did. When it became apparent that I couldn't look after the house, Mike also had to take over the domestic duties as well as going to work. On Saturdays he would go to the supermarket and get a week's shopping, and he started cooking meals in the evenings before he went to work. He also washed our clothes and tidied the house. It was a lot of responsibility resting on his shoulders, keeping the whole family together as well as dealing with his own grief.

The funny thing is that when I had something concrete that I had to do or when we had company, I could pull myself together. If we saw family or went to the pub with Jenny and Ian, I would laugh and joke along with the rest of the group and they would comment about what good form I was on. But as soon as they were gone, the black clouds descended once more. The same was true for my media work or campaigning for Sarah's Law, which I did with no problems as it gave me a focus. While cooking dinner was beyond me, I could easily get myself to London, Blackpool or Birmingham to speak at a conference on child safety or paedophilia – and increasingly did. In the months after the trial I spoke about Sarah's murder at a conference arranged by Ray Wyre Associates; attended the Victims of Crime Trust fundraiser; went to the Labour and Conservative Party conferences; as well as continuing to campaign for Sarah's Law with the *News of the World*.

I had expected the media attention to die down after Whiting's conviction, but the press continued to call for comments on every child safety issue from paedophilia to chat rooms to zebra crossings. It was at its worst when a child went missing. At these times we would be inundated with requests from both media and police for comments and advice and the phone would ring twenty or thirty times a day. As Mike had steadfastly refused to do any more media or campaigning work since the trial, I always took the calls when the press rang. If they asked for Mike to join me doing a conference, interview or photos, I didn't even bother to ask him, refusing on his behalf.

It wasn't that he no longer believed in Sarah's Law, it was just too hard for him to be actively involved. When I returned home after an interview or conference, Mike would ask me how it had gone. 'Fine,' I would reply.

Genuinely interested, he would press for details, asking, 'What did you talk about?'

I would reply vaguely, 'Oh, you know, Sarah's Law, the usual.' I think on some level I was punishing him for not coming with me, not being there for me. If he didn't want to come, he had forfeited his right to know about it.

Later that night on television, or the next day in the newspapers, Mike would inevitably see me standing on some stage addressing hundreds of people, looking calm and composed. The accompanying reports would often refer to me as 'brave' and 'strong'. They might add that Mike 'was too distraught' to appear or, just as bad, they wouldn't mention him at all. To Mike, the implication was that he was cowardly and weak for not being there. But we both knew the real story. Our public and private personas were so different. Yes, I could stand up and talk to a thousand people about Sarah's Law and have meetings with politicians, but I was incapable of washing the children's clothes and making dinner for my husband. To Mike, the woman he read about in the papers was a stranger. His wife at home was not brave or strong, she was scared and needed help doing the simplest things. With Mike it was the other way around. When he appeared on television he had red eyes and a haunted look, but at home he was the one keeping the family together. If one of us was the stronger, there was no question in my mind as to who it was.

Gradually, a silence grew up between us. Mike had given up trying to talk to me about anything as my responses were so deadened at that time, and eventually the dialogue between us pretty much stopped. In the old days we did everything together and knew each other's every feeling. If we had a problem, we would talk it through and deal with it as a unit. Now, we did less and less talking until we became virtual strangers. It got to the point where Mike would sometimes work seven days a week, just to be away from home. It was like a dark cloud had descended over the house and he would rather be anywhere but there.

Inevitably, after a long period of non-communication, Mike's frustration would build up so much that he would start a row, trying to provoke me into some sort of response. I think any sort of emotion would have done at that time, whether it was anger, grief or fear. He wanted me to strike out and slap him, or scream like I would have done before. He wanted something real from me, not this robot I had become. When Mike got really angry, usually late at night after a particularly heavy drinking session, he would threaten to walk out.

'I can't take this any more. I'm leaving!' he would shout.

'Come on, Mike,' I'd say wearily, 'calm down.'

'I'm serious, Sara, unless you tell me things are going to change, I'm going to walk out that door. Why can't you talk to me? I never know what you are thinking any more. I always have to second-guess you.'

But I couldn't tell him what I was thinking. I'm not sure that I even knew myself. Mike wanted me to fight for him and to fight for our marriage and I never did. While publicly I fought for change, the For Sarah campaign, privately there was no fight left in me.

In the summer of 2002, six months after the trial, when the situation at home was becoming desperate, Mike made a suggestion to get me out of my slump.

'Why don't you try going back to work?' he asked.

My first instinct was to say no. 'I can't face it,' I told him.

But Mike pushed, 'It'll do you good. You know you feel better when you're out of the house. And we could do with the extra cash.'

'I can't go back to the Old House,' I said. 'There are too many memories of Sarah.'

'It's not the only pub in the village. Kev is always saying he'll give you some shifts.'

Kevin was the landlord of the Barley Mow, the pub across the road from our house. He had often told me that if I wanted to work there he would give me a job, as I knew how to handle a bar and was friendly with all the regulars. He also said he would give me time off for any work I needed to do concerning Sarah's Law. I wouldn't get a better offer than that, so – after much debating – I decided to give it a go.

I was very nervous before my first shift, but I quickly got back into being behind the bar and slowly started to enjoy myself, serving drinks and chatting to the locals. It did me good to be out of the house, and for those hours it was like being transported back into my old life. Many of the pub regulars had been friends or acquaintances before Sarah was murdered, and to them I wasn't 'Sarah Payne's mother', I was just Sara. It did me good being with them. But the problem, as I soon discovered, was with strangers. As I started to work more regularly, I would catch people staring at me as I pulled pints. Some would recognise me straight away and tell me how sorry they were about Sarah or give an encouraging word for Sarah's Law. Others would say, 'Do I know you? I'm sure I recognise you from somewhere.' When the penny dropped, they would become embarrassed and start apologising.

I found it more and more difficult to be there, so when the pub closed for refurbishment in the autumn and a new landlord took over, I left. I could have got another job and there were even discussions about me working in the media. I had been told countless times that I was a natural on television and had also been offered newspaper columns to write. Having had children and married so young, it was tempting to have a go at a career of my own, but after a great deal of thought I decided against it. Media work would inevitably take me away from the family a great deal and I didn't want that. It wasn't just the children I was thinking of – it was me too. I worried when they were out of my sight for too long.

Then, in October 2002, my life took another blow when my brother Paul was taken ill. He had been suffering from chest pain and persistent coughing for some time and the doctors initially thought that he had pleurisy. But after a barrage of tests a tumour was found, and he was diagnosed with lung cancer. At first we were hopeful that he could be successfully operated on and live many more happy years. After all, he was only forty-four, healthy, ex-Army, and although he smoked, his habit was nowhere near as bad as the rest of ours. But when surgeons operated on him they found the cancer had spread. They couldn't tell us exactly how long he had, but the prognosis was not good. At first I simply couldn't deal with what was happening. I had lost my daughter and now I was going to lose my brother and there was nothing I could do about it. So I used my tried and tested method: I blocked it out. For the first weeks after his diagnosis, every time he was in hospital I would promise to go and see him but then make an excuse not to go at the last minute. It did not help that he lived in Sussex, which held such terrible memories.

Christmas came and Paul seemed to pick up a bit as his daughter arrived from Germany to see him, and he and his girlfriend Jackie made arrangements to get married. Not knowing how long Paul had left, they wanted to do it as soon as possible. Seeing him a bit better, I started to visit regularly and speak to him on the phone every other day, helping to make arrangements for his wedding that was scheduled for 15 January. But two days before he was to tie the knot, Paul suddenly came down with a nasty chest infection and had to be hospitalised. It quickly became clear that there was little the hospital could do for him, and he asked to be moved to a local hospice. The night before the wedding all the family were there with him at the hospice. He had picked up a bit, and we had a really enjoyable evening sitting around the smoking room – of all places – laughing, chatting and taking the mickey out of each other like nothing was wrong.

The next morning, Mum, my brother Johnny and I all went to Paul's house to pick up a couple of things for him for the big day. But there was no wedding. By the time we returned to the hospice Paul had died. My automatic response was to shut down again emotionally. I could almost physically feel the barriers coming up, never once crying as I busied myself with sorting out the practicalities and looking after Mum and Dad. As when Sarah died, I would not allow myself to grieve properly. Once again, I could not face giving into my emotions for fear they would overwhelm me. I simply went into myself a little bit more.

That winter, Charlotte turned eight – the age Sarah was when she died. Charlotte was five when her sister was killed, and although there was a strong family resemblance between them, the three-year age gap also meant they were quite different. They had different builds and Sarah always had a rounder face than her sister. Their personalities differed too: Sarah was the girlie soft one, and Charlotte was the wilful little madam. But now that Charlotte was eight she was more like Sarah in both looks and personality. Sometimes when I looked at her, it was like looking at a ghost.

She had also started at Bell Farm, Sarah's old school, and when I dropped her off in the mornings and picked her up in the evenings I was transported back in time to when I did the same for Sarah. I was also faced with seeing all Sarah's old friends, now eleven years old and growing bigger every day. Some days it made me so angry as I watched them spilling out of the school gates, as Sarah should have been there with them, giggling and laughing with her pals. It seemed so unfair that while her friends had futures, Sarah was frozen in time, for ever eight years old.

It wasn't just Charlotte's resemblance to Sarah that was the problem at that time, it was the general issue of her growing up and the problems it entailed. At the age of eight Charlotte had started to want more independence, which was very difficult for me. I had started letting her go to play at friends' houses after school again, but even though I knew there were adults present, I could not stop worrying about her. In the old days I would have used the time to myself to see a friend or do some shopping, but now I stayed at home texting or calling constantly. One day I forced myself to let Lee take her fishing to the local lake, and another day Luke took her to the park. But it wasn't enough for her, and she began to ask if she could play out the front or go to the shops with her friends.

'Mummy, please, please, please can me and Mazie go and buy some sweets?'

'I'll take you in a minute, sweetheart,' I'd say.

'But we want to go on our own,' she would whine.

'I don't think so.'

'But the other girls in my class are allowed. I'm not a baby any more,' she'd say, feeling frustrated. 'You'll have to let me at some time.'

'I know, I will, but not yet.'

If Sarah had still been alive, I'm sure I would have let them go out together, but after what had happened I just couldn't bring myself to let her out alone. I knew that being over-protective wasn't doing her any good in the long run, but I couldn't help it. I couldn't even bring myself to wait for her outside the school gates at night, like she wanted. I had to go inside every day. She tried desperately to get me to compromise – meeting her halfway – but I couldn't even do this. I hadn't been able to protect Sarah, and I wasn't going to let it happen twice.

Meanwhile, our domestic situation also took a turn for the worse, when Mike was taken off the night shift and started working days. It was a disaster for him, as he had built up a great relationship with the lads on nights and they had become a close-knit team. They knew Mike well enough to know when to leave him alone and when he wanted to talk, and if he had been in the papers they wouldn't mention it unless he did first. Now he had to start over again. Some days, if anything relating to Sarah had been in the news, they would greet Mike with the words: 'Here's our celebrity!' They didn't mean anything by it, they were just having a joke, but to Mike it was far from funny.

11

PREGNANCY

I had thought that everything would be different – better – after Whiting was put away, but I came to realise that it made little difference. It didn't make my pain any less. The fact remained that my daughter had been killed in the most horrible way and there was no getting over that, no making it better. I could only hope that I would learn to live with the fact better than I had been doing.

Soon the spring came, but the dark clouds didn't lift in the house. One day in March I woke up feeling sick and exhausted, as if I hadn't slept at all. All I wanted to do was turn over and go back to sleep until lunchtime, but I couldn't, as I had to take Charlotte to school. I hauled myself out of bed and wandered into the bathroom. Perhaps a shower would wake me up and make me feel better. But as I turned the water on, a great wave of nausea suddenly swept over me and I just had time to put my head over the basin, before being violently sick.

'Are you OK?' shouted Lee.

I gasped for breath. 'Just feeling a bit ill, I'll be fine,' I reassured him, before retching again.

Slowly, when there was nothing left inside me, I started to feel better. Walking down to the kitchen I put the kettle on. There were two empty wine bottles on the side that I had polished off the night before. Just looking at them made me feel sick again and I resolved, not for the first time, that I really had to cut down on my drinking.

Over the next couple of weeks I tried to drink less. It wasn't hard, as every time I had more than a couple of pints or glasses of wine I was sick. One evening, after a few in the pub with Mike, I rushed to the bathroom with my hand to my mouth as soon as we got home. When I emerged, pale faced, ten minutes later Mike joked, 'You're not pregnant, are you?'

'Yeah, right,' I laughed weakly.

Neither of us seriously thought I could be. For a start, our sex life, like our relationship in general, had steadily deteriorated since Sarah's death. Also, I had never suffered from sickness when pregnant, so it was far more likely to be the alcohol or a stomach bug. I was sure it would pass.

I wasn't the only one feeling under the weather at that time. Mike's depression was worse than it had been in a long while. He was taking his medication, but all the alcohol he was drinking was making it less effective. Mike had been feeling down before he swapped from nights to days, but at least then he had the understanding of his friends from work. Now that his support structure had gone, he was finding it increasingly difficult to get up and go to work in the mornings. When he started waking up literally shaking from head to toe, he began to take the odd day off. After seeing his doctor, it was decided that he should take a bit of time out to recover and he was signed off sick. With us both at home all day and night, feeling physically and emotionally low, it was a recipe for disaster.

A month later I still felt no better, so I decided to get myself checked out by the doctor. By now a nagging doubt had started up in the back of my mind. *Could* I be pregnant? I tried to think when my last period had been, but I had no idea, not being the type of woman who keeps records of her cycles in a diary. On the day of my doctor's appointment on 17 April I decided to buy a home pregnancy test, going to the chemist when Mike had gone to the pub at lunchtime. It showed how much our relationship had changed, as previously I would have told him my suspicions and we would have bought and done the test together. Now, as I took the box out of the paper bag in the bathroom at home, I was all alone.

I had done pregnancy tests numerous times over the years and it was a routine I was familiar with. What I wasn't familiar with were my feelings. I was filled with dread at the thought of a positive result, a feeling I hadn't even had when I had done my first pregnancy test at the age of seventeen. All my past pregnancies had been happy events, but now – as I waited for the results of the test, I found myself praying for it to be negative.

After Sarah's murder Mike and I had occasionally discussed having another child. Sometimes when he saw a baby he would get broody and say, 'Come on, Sara, let's have another one,' but I was adamant that I didn't want to. In a general sense, I couldn't face bringing another child into a world such as ours, where paedophiles can snatch them off the streets. More specifically, I didn't think it was fair to bring a child into our family. It would be so hard for them to grow up with the shadow of Sarah hanging over them, a big sister they had never known but everybody else did.

The result showed up in less than a minute: that tell-tale little blue line. I was pregnant. 'Oh my God, no, no, no,' I said out loud, sitting on the edge of the bath. There has to be some mistake, I thought, these tests can be wrong, can't they? I looked at my watch. It was nearly time for my doctor's appointment. Maybe he would tell me it wasn't true.

With that tiny hope in mind, I rushed off to the surgery, but the doctor didn't even bother doing another test.

'Home tests are nearly 100 per cent accurate these days, Sara,' he told me. 'How do you feel about it?'

'I can't. I can't have another child,' I said, desperation creeping into my voice.

I explained to him that Sarah's death had made having another child too difficult for me. There were also other problems. Mike and I were arguing all the time, I had been drinking and smoking too heavily and wasn't healthy, and there would be a huge age gap between this child and the rest of the children. All in all, I told the doctor, everything pointed towards me not having this baby.

'If that's really how you feel, I can book you an appointment at the clinic and they can talk you through your options.'

I nodded. 'Yes please.'

The word wasn't said, but it hung in the air between us: abortion. I have always been pro-choice, as I believe it is every woman's right to choose for herself whether to have a baby, but it was not something I had ever considered for myself before. Now it seemed like my only option.

I was in a daze for the rest of the day, going through the motions of picking Charlotte up from school. Later, as I sat in the front room waiting for Mike to come in, I tried to work out when the baby had been conceived. I could only think of one occasion when Mike and I had been intimate over the last few months. At the end of February there had been a fundraiser event for the Victims of Crime Trust, which I had become active in, and – unusually – Mike had come with me. There were no interviews or speeches to be done and, for the first time in a long while, we had really enjoyed ourselves and it had felt right being together at the end of the night. As I sat lost in my thoughts, I heard the key turn in the lock and Mike appeared. I didn't even wait for him to say hello, blurting out, 'I've been to the doctor's today.'

Seeing my look, Mike started to ask if I was all right, but I cut him off.

'I'm pregnant,' I stated.

He nodded silently, calmer than me. I didn't give him a chance to say anything.

'I can't have it. We can't. The doctor's made an appointment with the clinic,' I babbled.

'If that's what you want . . .' Mike began, before Charlotte ran into the room.

'Mum, I'm hungry,' she whined, 'can I have a Happy Meal?'

Mike and I looked at each other and I said, 'Daddy will take you.'

My date with the clinic was scheduled for 24 April, but my doctor called at the last minute. He was concerned that the place was too public and that I might be recognised there, which was the last thing I needed, so another appointment was made for me at a clinic in London. It meant having to wait another few days, but it seemed like a more sensible idea. During those days of waiting I was like a runaway train. Although Mike tried to discuss the matter with me several times, I refused to talk about it. My mind was made up. I wasn't going through with the pregnancy. It helped when I thought of it like that: as a pregnancy, not a baby. I carried on smoking and drinking, although the alcohol often made me sick, and continued to skip meals or eat greasy take-aways. There was no point changing my lifestyle under the circumstances.

On the day of my appointment Mike and I travelled up to London on the train. I didn't really know what to expect at the clinic, as it hadn't been explained to me what would happen, and I felt sick with nerves. Once there, we saw a doctor who confirmed my pregnancy with another test and then did a scan. As I lay on the table and she applied gel and then moved the scanner over my still flat stomach, she said, 'It looks like you're about nine and a half weeks gone.' I nodded dully. 'Do you want to see?' she asked, but I shook my head, which was turned away from the monitor. Seeing a baby – no matter how tiny – would make it all too real. I told the doctor that we wanted to terminate the pregnancy and she said that it could be arranged, advising us to see one of their counsellors first, which we did, explaining our reasons for not wanting to have another child. Everybody there was very supportive and understanding and we were never made to feel bad about our decision. When an appointment was made for me to have an abortion the next week, I was sure it was the right thing to do.

The next day, as I sat watching daytime television and trying to block out my life, my eyes kept being drawn back to the big white envelope I had been given the day before at the clinic. I had been told to take it with me to my next appointment. I idly picked it up and opened the flap, taking out a few sheets of paper. Something fluttered to the floor and fell face down. As I picked it up and turned it over, I saw with a shock that it was my scan picture. I had refused to look at it the day before but now that it was in my hand I couldn't resist. As I stared at the black and white image, I could pick out a tiny shape. It was my baby. I slowly put my hand to my stomach, and I smiled.

When Mike got home from the pub that night he looked even more miserable than usual. As the children got ready for bed and Mike and I watched television, he suddenly blurted out, 'I don't want us to do this. If you're determined I'll be there for you, but it's not what I want.'

Relief flooded over me. 'Neither do I! I don't know who I was trying to kid. I can't get rid of our baby.'

And, for the first time in ages, we gave each other a hug.

'Let's tell the kids,' Mike said smiling, and I nodded happily, although I was a bit apprehensive about how they would react.

We gathered the children together and I took a deep breath.

'We've got something to tell you,' I said, as they looked at me expectantly, 'I'm having a baby. You're going to have a brother or sister.'

They all broke into beaming smiles.

'I want a sister!' Charlotte squealed.

'No, I want a brother,' said Lee.

'I don't mind,' piped up Luke.

I was bowled over by their reactions and I thought, for the hundredth time, how lucky I was to have them.

For a few days after we had made our decision everything seemed back on track as the new baby reunited the family. All the things I had worried about when I discovered I was pregnant suddenly didn't any longer seem so important. I wanted to keep the news quiet until I was a bit further along, but Mike couldn't contain himself and wanted to shout it from the rooftops. He kept telling people and swearing them to secrecy, but before long the whole village was talking about it.

As the news filtered out, we knew we had to make a decision about going public with the pregnancy. The media would get hold of the story sooner or later and we decided that we would rather the news came from us. We didn't want a massive fuss, so we decided to do just one piece and I contacted the *News of the World* who came to see us. I did the interview and the photos, and Mike agreed to give one quote. He hadn't done any media work in a long time, but we both felt it would look very odd if he said nothing about the happy news. After the article was printed we naively thought that we could forget about it, but we were wrong, as the following day the phone started ringing off the hook again. As I fielded calls, some of the old pressures and problems came back, and I could feel the tension building once more between Mike and me.

Ten days later, on 13 May, I was due to speak at the Police Federation Conference in Blackpool about Sarah's Law. By now, under the direction of David Blunkett, a substantial number of new measures had been made law. Yet there was still the most important, central part of Sarah's Law to push: the right to controlled access. Although Rebekah Wade had left the *News of the World* to edit the *Sun* in January, the new editor Andy Coulson had confirmed that the paper would remain committed to campaigning for Sarah's Law, for which we were very grateful.

I had agreed to make the speech before I knew I was pregnant, but I didn't see why the baby should stop me. I had been feeling tired and unwell, and I knew that the long day would tire me, but Hayley and Stuart from the *News of the World* were going to travel with me on the train and we would not stay for the evening do. Although Mike had been invited, as always, he didn't even consider it.

As we pulled out of London I felt a little apprehensive about the day ahead. I would be addressing an audience of 1,000 police officers, by far the largest crowd I had ever spoken to, and it was slightly daunting. Hayley interrupted my thoughts, asking, 'Can I see your speech?'

'You know I don't write speeches, Hayley,' I laughed.

'You mean you've written nothing down at all?' she asked, incredulous. 'This isn't a two-minute press conference, you know.'

'I know,' I said simply, 'but I've told you a hundred times, when I write things down I choke on my words. Don't worry, I know roughly what I want to say. It'll be fine.'

Hayley shook her head, sighing, 'Your choice.'

When we walked into the packed ballroom of Blackpool's Winter Gardens I was overwhelmed. As I took a seat facing the stage I recalled seeing politicians on television standing on the very same platform making speeches, and now I was about to do the same. Three years ago such a thing would have been unthinkable for me and it made me realise just how much my life had changed. When I was introduced, I took a deep breath and strode to the stage, looking far more composed than I felt. Standing at the podium, I began. I didn't know what I was going to say until I started.

'Hello. I'm often asked to speak and I drive people mad because I won't write speeches. I won't speak anybody else's words, so anything I say comes from the heart and is, as far as I'm concerned, the truth.

'Why am I here? I'm here because I was part of what I thought was a very normal family, we had a large family, a loud family. We went to visit my mother and father-in-law for a weekend. The children asked if they could go out to play, it was sunny, it was hot, the cornfield is less than 50 yards away from the house. Idyllic, some people may say. We went for a walk down on the beach, the children played on the beach for a little while, they went back to the field.

'At about 8 o'clock, in fact it was earlier than that, we couldn't find Sarah. She had just disappeared from view and, as I am sure any parent would who has lost sight of their child on numerous occasions without thought, you immediately panic.

It doesn't matter who you are or how big or strong you are, you panic.

'We searched for the first five minutes, not really worrying too much, thinking she was hiding. We continued to search, we ran up and down, in and out of the field, down to the sea, every field we could find, stopped every person we could stop. And there weren't that many around, believe it or not, but every single person stopped, helped us look, went back over their steps, came back to us and started again. When it began to get dark, I grew frightened for my daughter. She's very scared of the dark – hates it.

'We searched one more time and rang the police. We said she was eight, alone, and she'd be scared. Thank God the police acted in such a courageous way at that moment, they had the helicopters out, and by morning there were thousands searching. Every policeman had given up his time off and, I can tell you, had it not been for you guys I wouldn't have got my daughter back. OK, it wasn't in the circumstances we wanted, but we got her home; there are many out there that didn't. So I'd like to thank you guys and I'd like to say what a brilliant job you do. You do the best you can and I know that each and every one of you puts children first. Anything we say or we do is not against you.

'This is about trying to make changes for the better, some people may agree and some people may not. That's up to you. What I'm saying is, give me an alternative. Because I tell you something, if I had known Roy Whiting had lived in that area, there's no way my children would have been out to play. I'm not that over-protective – OK, some might say I am a bit, but no more than any other parent. That information would have saved my daughter's life. All that I can say is, how many lives would that have saved just by giving it a second thought. When you make changes like this you never know how many lives you save because it's the ones that aren't hurt who are the ones that are saved. All that you can go by is numbers: do they go down, do they go up, we don't know.

'Naming and Shaming was hard. When the groups rioted, it was hard. We felt very responsible, but we knew we were doing the right thing. Most of us at that point lived with our heads totally in the clouds when it came to sex offenders. I assumed that if somebody hurt a child, they went to prison. I assumed that they were on a register when they came out of prison, that the police had resources to look after them, that probation wouldn't let them out of prison unless they were damn sure they weren't going to re-offend. I've learnt so many things that horrify me and scare me as a parent. Children can't look after themselves, it's up to us as adults, and I hope that we all try our very best.

'Naming and Shaming carried on with mine and Michael's full support, and I have to say that the *News of the World* team rang us on a daily basis to see if we wanted to stop or halt, or if we wanted to withdraw our support. We never said that we would, and we never did. I still support that campaign because without it nobody would have listened to Sara Payne, mother of Sarah Payne. They would have said: "Knee-jerk reaction, poor woman, there, there, sorry she's been hurt, sorry your daughter is dead, but there is nothing we can do."

'Well, I'm telling the government there *is* something you can do, you can give parents the power to look after their children. I'm not asking for the register to be open, I'm not asking to know about every flasher, every family member that is molested, every groomer. I think there are better people than me to say whether these people should or shouldn't be told.

'What I am saying is that if you cannot keep Roy Whiting in prison, if you're going to let him out as an experiment to see whether he does it again, when every agency in the world is screaming at you, "This man is going to re-offend and you're going to let him out early," then you damn well better make sure the community at least knows that he's around. Whether that be by his name, by his address, or whether that is simply by answering a personal question when a parent walks into a police station and says: "Is there a risk round here? Is there a risk to my child to go and play down on the beach? Should I be wary?"

'Well, the answer is of course that in most places in Britain, as I'm sure most of you know, yes there's always a certain risk. But when you have a predator in your midst, that risk is high, very high. So yes, if we can get indeterminate sentencing in, there's no need for Sarah's Law. If we can get life to mean life, and when I say life I mean the whole of your natural life, then, yeah, there's no need. But we all know that the European Court will not allow that, they will not allow it, they will not allow us to lock them up and throw away the key. It isn't how it works and it isn't how we work as human beings.

'There are lots of schemes that have been put forward, the Buddy scheme for instance, which I am very interested in supporting. But as we all know, that takes money, it takes volunteers, and it takes a lot of strong characters to carry that out. I just want to give you a thought. Sarah would be alive if I'd known that Roy Whiting was there.

'But my final thought is that when Roy Whiting is released from prison, he doesn't go on the sex offenders' register; he's a murderer and child abductor and that means he doesn't go on the register. That means that Sarah's Law doesn't count in his case. He killed my daughter and one day he will face probation. And I'm sure that the powers that be will say enough time has passed and he's paid his penalty. What I say is that my grandchildren, my future grandchildren, are at a real risk from men like this and we have to find a way of protecting our children. Thank you.'

After I had finished there were a few moments' silence before the clapping began. Slowly, the officers around the hall rose to their feet and the sound of their applause touched me like nothing else. To know that they were behind Sarah's Law meant a huge amount to me as the police had done so much for my family. We had always found that bobbies on the beat supported us, and now it seemed we also had the support of some of the highest-ranking officers in Britain.

The next morning, after spending the night in Blackpool, Stuart, Hayley and I made our way back to the station, where we got a train to Preston, to change for London. At Preston, Stuart went ahead to find out what time our train was, while Hayley and I started walking over the bridge to the other platform. Halfway across I suddenly felt very weak, and I reached out for Hayley to support me. Then I felt a warm wet sensation down below and I wondered briefly if my waters had broken prematurely. But as I reached down, my hand came back bright red. My clothes were soaked through with blood, which was now dripping on to the floor. 'Oh my God, the baby,' I gasped. Hayley quickly took control of the situation, wrapping her coat around me, and saying, 'Don't panic. Let's get you to the bathroom.' As she supported me to the ladies, she got her mobile out and rang for an ambulance, telling them to come quickly.

As I sat in the ladies' toilets on the platform station, blood still seeping out of me, I was beside myself. I had just accepted that I was pregnant, and now it looked as if I was going to lose my baby. I couldn't bear the thought. Taking out my phone, I tried to ring Mike. He doesn't have a mobile, but it had become our habit, when I was away, for him to carry Lee's phone in case

I needed him urgently. I never had done before, and now that I did Lee's phone just rang and rang. Ending the call with a curse, I closed my eyes. I'm not sure that I had ever prayed before, but it was a measure of how desperate I was that I did. 'Please don't take this baby away too,' I implored a God I wasn't even sure existed. 'I'll do anything, just don't take my baby. I can't stand it again.'

The ambulance arrived within a few minutes and I was whisked off to the hospital where a doctor examined me. As he did so, I kept asking him, 'Have I lost my baby?'

'I'm sorry, Sara,' he said shaking his head, 'but I can't tell you that yet. We need to do more tests. I'm going to have to transfer you to another hospital for a scan.'

So I was put back in the ambulance and taken to a nearby hospital, with Hayley and Stuart following behind. Once there, I was taken for a scan. Studying the monitor the doctor looked puzzled.

'I've lost it, haven't I?' I asked him.

'I'm not sure what's going on,' he said honestly. 'I'm going to call for a second opinion.'

Another doctor was called to have a look, and they pointed at the screen, conferring in low voices. By now I was getting more and more anxious.

'What is it? What's wrong?' I asked.

And then the doctor dropped the bombshell. 'Did you know that you were expecting twins?' he asked me.

My mind reeled. Twins?

'No,' I said weakly.

'It's easy to miss on an early scan,' he said, 'especially with non-identical twins.'

As the doctor was still speaking, his earlier words came back to me.

'You said I *was* expecting twins. Are they gone?'

'Look at the monitor,' he said. 'Can you see this dark flat area? It looks as if you've lost one of the babies. I'm sorry.'

'Will the other baby be OK?' I asked immediately.

'There's no reason to think it shouldn't be fine. We need to keep you in overnight for observation.'

It was a lot to take in, but my initial feeling was one of relief. I was still having a baby. I tried to be philosophical about the one I had lost, and the fact that I had never known it existed made it easier. I had had two miscarriages before and I knew that these things happened for a reason. It is nature's way of saying that something's wrong. As I lay there taking in the news, I thought: one baby for me, one for Sarah.

After the doctor left, Hayley and Stuart came in and I told them what had happened. They were very supportive, and arranged to stay in a local hotel so they would be nearby and could take me back home the next day. When I felt strong enough, I got out of bed and walked to the front of the hospital to call Mike on my mobile. This time he picked up the phone on the first ring.

'All right, love?'

'Not really. I'm in Preston – in hospital.'

'What's happened? Is it the baby?'

My voice broke. 'Mike, it was twins. We've lost one.'

There was a silence on the other end of the line for a moment, before Mike asked, 'What about the other one?'

'The doctor says it should be fine.'

'Do you need me to come up?'

'There's no point, I can come home tomorrow. I'll see you then.'

'Will you call me later?' he asked, and I told him I would.

I went back to the ward and got into bed again. Going over my conversation with Mike in my mind, I suddenly felt very alone. If anything like this had happened before, it would have been so different. For a start, we wouldn't have been apart in the first place. If we had, there wouldn't have been any question as to whether Mike would have come up. He would have been on the first train and I would have been counting the minutes until he arrived.

I was awake most of the night, going over the day's events in my mind. Like when Sarah was taken, I blamed myself. I had drunk a lot in the early stages of my pregnancy and I had been feeling tired and ill. I should have listened to my body and not pushed myself. If I hadn't pushed myself, then perhaps I wouldn't have lost one of my babies. The doctor told me that there was no point looking for reasons and I tried to tell myself that if the baby wasn't meant to come into this world, then there was nothing I could have done about it. If I hadn't miscarried that day, it might have been the next day or week. But as much as I repeated this to myself, I still felt guilty.

The next day the doctor came round and told me that I could go home, telling me to rest and not overdo it. Hayley got us a taxi to the station and we got the train back to London where a car picked me up to take me back home. As I walked through the door Mike greeted me in the hall and gave me a big hug, but as he held me, something felt wrong. I should have felt safe and reassured to be back in his arms, but I didn't. I felt like our connection had gone again and all the problems that had overwhelmed me when I first found out I was pregnant suddenly flooded back. Pulling away from him, I said, 'I'm going to lie down. The doctor says I need to take it easy.'

He nodded. 'You go up. I'll bring you a cup of tea.'

12

THE SEPARATION

Over the next few days the bleeding slowed down, and I began to regain some of my strength. The experience had been a real wake-up call for me and I vowed that I would start looking after myself better. I couldn't carry on selfishly as I had been, I had to start considering my baby and putting it first. I was going to cut down on the cigarettes, have a healthier diet, and not put myself under undue stress. Perhaps most importantly, I had to stop drinking.

We have always been a family who drink a lot. With Terry and Les, and Mike for a time, working in off-licences, there had always been alcohol around us, and we all used it to socialise and unwind. After Sarah's death it had become a crutch that propped us up. With a few drinks inside us, the pain of our daughter's death didn't shine quite so harshly. It soon became part of our everyday routine and there was barely a day since Sarah had been taken that we hadn't drank. It had become as normal as eating or sleeping.

When I stopped drinking, my pregnant body was grateful, as

the alcohol was making me physically sick. Sober, my mind also got healthier, and I started to see things more clearly. With Mike not working, we had started spending all our days in the pub, a habit that we carried on even when I was no longer drinking. It was simply to get us out of the house and provide us with some company. As Mike sat drinking pint after pint, while I stuck to soft drinks, I watched his mood change. I had never really been aware of the process before, as I had always been going through it myself. While tipsy in the pub he would be quite jolly and fun to be around, but by the time we got home he was drunk, aggressive and confrontational, itching for a fight. Some nights when he started ranting, I would say, 'Shut up, Mike, you're drunk.' Yet even as I said the words I felt like such a hypocrite, as I would be doing exactly the same if I weren't pregnant.

Given that we had all day every day together we could have got out of the pub and used our time constructively. We could have done the shopping or cooking, or sorted out the house, but we never did. In the past we had been such a good team, a real partnership, but since Sarah's death we had grown further and further apart. It was obvious in so many little ways. Before, in the evenings we might cook a big chilli together in the kitchen, me chopping the onions, Mike frying the mince, while we listened to music and had a couple of glasses of wine. I could hardly remember us doing that over the past three years. It had got to the point where, after a day sitting in the pub, Mike would cook silently in the kitchen, while I sat watching television.

Even the children could tell that the bond between us was weakening. We had always had a policy when it came to the kids that we stuck together in our decisions. If Mike said that they couldn't do something I would always back him up, whether I thought he was right or not, and vice versa. We had always presented ourselves as one solid unit, but increasingly I almost took pleasure in contradicting Mike for the sake of it and undermining his authority with the children.

Before long, we started to argue every night. The rows would always start off about petty things and escalate into bigger issues. A chat about cooking tea could end with one of us shouting at the other one to get out of the house and never come back. There was nothing constructive about the fights, we were just trying to hurt one another as much as possible. Increasingly, we would go to bed angry and not speaking to each other and wake up in the mornings feeling hurt and guilty. On a good day we would apologise for the things we had said the night before and try to start again. On a bad one we didn't even do that, we just ignored each other. This was the worst of all. At least when we were fighting it was a form of communication.

One day, towards the end of July, we had a row that was typical for us at the time. I had picked Charlotte up from school while Mike stayed on at the pub. When he came home later, drunk, he tripped over a bike in the driveway and from inside the house I heard him swear. As he came through the front door he called out sarcastically, 'Honey, I'm home. What's for tea?'

Staring at the television and trying to ignore his tone, I said, 'Dunno, I've not thought about it. What do you want?'

He snapped back, 'Can't you ever decide on your own? Let's look in the fridge, shall we?'

I walked behind him into the kitchen, knowing what he would find when he opened the fridge: nothing.

'Ah, you've not done the shopping either then,' he stated.

'I've not had the chance,' I replied wearily.

'Why not? You're not exactly busy, are you?'

'I just didn't get round to it. What's the big deal? Let's have a take-away.'

'I'm sick of bloody take-aways. You don't do anything around here.'

'You're not working. Do it yourself,' I replied.

'I already do everything,' he exploded. 'What's wrong with you?'

I shrugged my shoulders.

'Talk to me. What's going on?'

I looked steadfastly at the floor and refused to meet his eye. If there was one thing that really annoyed Mike, it was when I refused to speak.

'Sara! Hello, is anyone there? Speak!'

'What's the point?' I replied.

'I'm beginning to wonder,' shouted Mike. 'Are you trying to drive me away? Because you're doing a good job of it. If you don't want me any more, then say so, because I can't stand this. Do you want a divorce?'

I shook my head. 'I don't know what I want.'

'Well, you'd better decide,' Mike said as he slammed the fridge and stomped upstairs.

The fight wasn't any different to a hundred we'd had before, but somehow it was one too many, the straw that broke the camel's back. As we lay in bed that night, our backs turned on each other, I mulled things over in my head. Mike and I had never had a perfect marriage. Both passionate, feisty people, we had always had our ups and downs, but we always got through them because we had a solid foundation of love and under-standing. But after Sarah's death our cement had gradually begun to crack until it was almost beyond repair. With each fight we were simply alienating one other more and more. If it carried on for much longer we would end up hating each other and I couldn't let that happen. There was also another thing to consider: the baby. We couldn't bring a new baby into that house, with the constant fighting, the mess, and the bad atmosphere. Being pregnant and sober helped me come to a decision that should have been made months before. I had no idea whether it would be for ever or as a temporary measure, but we had to separate.

After taking Charlotte to school the next day, I told Mike that I needed to speak to him. Once we were sitting in the front room, I said without any preamble, 'As soon as I can get some money together I'm going to move out.'

For once, it was Mike who was silent. We had often bandied the words 'separation' and 'divorce' about in anger or drunkenness, but not in the cold light of day, so it was obviously a shock to him.

I carried on. 'We both know we can't carry on like this. Something's got to change.'

'So that's it? Our marriage is over?' he asked.

'I don't know,' I said honestly, 'I just know that we're making each other, and everyone around us, miserable. I think we need some time apart, to get our heads together and think about what we want.'

Mike nodded. Part of me wanted him to beg me to reconsider, but he didn't. I don't know whether it was pride that stopped him or whether he knew as well as I did that it was the right decision.

'If that's what you want, fine. I'll sleep downstairs until you find a place.'

That night Mike slept on the sofa, and the night after that he made up a bed in the back room. We told the children that we were having a few problems, but they were used to us fighting by now, and assumed that we would sort it out. Luke would come in from school and say jokingly, 'Are you two all right now?' Everyone seemed certain that we would sort it out in the end.

Our family and friends had seen our marriage go through bad patches over the years and we had always come out the other side. They thought, 'It's just Mike and Sara being silly, they'll be fine.' I had always thought that in the past too, but this time I wasn't so sure.

Just days after Mike and I started sleeping in separate beds, on 31 July, I was due to go to the hospital for a scan. It was a nerve-racking day as it would tell me whether the baby was healthy and, after the miscarriage, I obviously feared the worst. The scan would also reveal the baby's sex, which I felt ambiguous about. It should have been a day where Mike and I pulled together and gave each other some support, but we were too far gone for that. Mike wanted to be there, as it was his baby too, but as we drove to the hospital we were distant towards each other. Charlotte had insisted on coming along with us, as she was so excited about the new baby, and as she sat in the back chattering away animatedly with Mazie, she didn't seem to notice the tension between her parents.

As we pulled into St Peter's hospital in Chertsey I felt a pang. It was where Sarah had been born and my mind flashed briefly back to arriving in the ambulance, blue lights flashing. I had wanted Mike with me so much that night, and now I didn't care if he was with me or not. In the hospital, I changed into a blue robe and Charlotte watched, fascinated, as the nurse put gel on my tummy, moved the scanner over it, and the baby popped up on the screen. Reminded of the last time I had a scan, I said quickly, 'Is everything OK?'

The nurse peered at the screen before answering. 'Everything seems fine. The baby's sitting quite low down, so it's hard to see the facial features, but it looks medium sized and healthy.'

I breathed a sigh of relief when she added, after closer

inspection, that its heart, brain and spine were all as they should be.

The hospital doesn't automatically tell you if you are having a boy or a girl, so when everything else had been checked I asked, 'Can you tell us the sex?'

The nurse had a closer look and said, 'I'm 95 per cent certain it's a little girl.'

Charlotte, who had been longing for a sister, clapped her hands and a beaming smile came over her face. After the gel had been wiped off, she patted my tummy and said, 'Hello, little sister.' She repeated the ritual before she went to bed that night, saying, 'Goodnight, little sister.' It was always Sarah who was the soft one, but the baby seemed to have brought out the maternal instinct in Charlotte. She had really missed having a sister around, and although the new baby could never replace Sarah – for Charlotte or for any of us – I knew it would be nice for her to have another girl in the house.

While Charlotte was ecstatic at the news, I was confused. Although I had not expressed the wish out loud, I had privately been hoping for a boy. Having a girl seemed so much more complicated, so fraught with problems, both for us as a family and the child itself. One of my main worries was that my new daughter would look just like Sarah, as there are quite strong resemblances between the siblings in our family. Lee and Luke have always looked alike and Sarah and Charlotte did, so there was bound to be a likeness between Sarah and this baby. I didn't know if I could stand people constantly making the comparison between their looks and personalities, as I wanted her to be her own person from the start, not living in Sarah's shadow.

Another anxiety was that I would be too over-protective of her. When the other children were growing up I was a pretty laid-back mum, but after Sarah's death that changed. Three years after her murder I could still hardly bear to let Charlotte out of my sight, so how would I be with a helpless baby? Would I ever be able to relax and put my feelings on the back burner and let her grow up normally? I knew a balance would have to be found between protecting her and giving her the freedom to live her own life. In the past I would have talked my fears over with Mike and we would have discussed ways of making the situation easier, but by that time we couldn't discuss anything without it turning into an argument.

After Mike and I had made the decision to split up we started fighting less, but the atmosphere in the house was terrible. For a couple who had been inseparable, sleeping in different beds was heart-breaking, and an awful sadness descended upon us. On our thirteenth wedding anniversary on 4 August we weren't even speaking to each other and we were coming to realise that we could not continue to live separate lives under the same roof. The problem was that I had no money to move out, and no family to stay with where I would still be near the children.

Luckily, the situation was solved for us when Mike was made redundant on 12 August. With some money behind him from the redundancy package, we decided that it was more practical for him to move out.

'It will still be your house too,' I told him. 'You can come over and see me and the children whenever you want. And we'll see each other with Jenny and Ian, and in the pub. Things won't be that different, it's just that you won't be living here.'

But he warned me, 'We're either together or we're not, Sara. If I move out, then that's it. I'm not being one of those live-out husbands.'

I nodded, but it tore me apart inside. I wanted to have my cake and eat it: to have some time and space to myself, and to have Mike available to me and the children when I needed him.

Mike started looking for somewhere else to live immediately and just a few days later he saw a room advertised in the local paper, lodging in a family house down the road. As he walked out of the door to go and look at the room I told him not to take it if it wasn't suitable, as I didn't want him living somewhere horrible. But although not ideal, it was nice enough, and he took it on the spot. The owners told him he could move in as soon as he liked and we decided there was no point prolonging the agony. I couldn't bear to help him pack his bags, so I sat downstairs while he threw his clothes into a suitcase. As he packed, Jenny popped round and said to me, frustrated, 'Why don't you just give each other a big cuddle and forget it?' And right to the last minute part of me expected one of us to cave in and put a stop to it all, but we didn't – we had gone past that point.

Before Mike left that evening, we had to tell the children what was happening. They had done a good job ignoring the situation so far, thinking that they would come home from school one day and it would all be fine. We had been delaying telling them that it wasn't, but there could be no more stalling now. Sitting them down, I said, 'You know that we have been fighting a lot recently and it's not been very nice for anybody. Well, we think it would be best if Dad moves out.'

After this had sunk in for a minute, Lee asked, 'Does this mean you're getting divorced?'

'No,' I said, 'We're not talking about that. We just need a bit of time apart.'

Charlotte piped up, 'Will I still see Daddy?'

Mike took her on his knee, shaking with emotion. 'I'm only going up the road. You'll still see me all the time, I promise.'

Luke, ever practical, asked, 'Does this mean you'll stop fighting so much?'

I told him truthfully, 'We certainly hope so, yes.'

When we told our parents and the rest of the family the news, they were very sad. But they didn't try to talk us round as they could see how we had been tearing each other apart. Their view was: 'If you can work this out and be happy together that's great, but if you can't, then put an end to it now.'

On the night that Mike left there were so many conflicting emotions going round in my head. On the one hand, I felt terribly alone and abandoned, subconsciously waiting for his key to turn in the lock. Mike and I had slept in the same bed almost every night for nearly twenty years, and now we didn't even live in the same house. It was very scary and I wondered how I would cope without him. Yet there was a small part of me that felt relieved. At least now there would be no more screaming matches before bedtime, no more tension in the house, nobody to shout at me when the household chores hadn't been done. Part of me felt free.

The hardest part of moving out for Mike was not seeing the children regularly. He had always been very involved in their lives, a real hands-on dad, and he missed the hustle and bustle of everyday family life. Yet he was reluctant to have them visit him in his new room, as it was just that: a room. He didn't even have a kitchen of his own to make them some tea. He talked about getting a proper place, a flat where he could have them over to stay, but I was reluctant. It made everything so much more final; it was the next stage in our separation and I wasn't ready for that. So we compromised, agreeing that he should start dropping by the house every day to see the children.

I knew after Mike left that I had to start turning my life around. Mike's moving out would stop the constant fighting, but it wouldn't magically cure all the family's problems. The state of the house, the mess, lack of routine, and my general depression were all issues that had to be addressed. I decided to start with the most manageable tasks – getting my physical surroundings in order and the family back into some sort of normal routine. While Mike was at home there was always an excuse for me to do nothing, as if I just left things long enough then eventually he would do them. But now that he was gone, if I didn't do the shopping, then the children would go hungry and I couldn't have that.

I didn't kid myself that I was going to become a perfect housewife and mother immediately – or perhaps ever – but I started with little steps. The first positive thing I did was to make a conscious effort not to turn the television on in the daytime. Instead I would sit down after taking Charlotte to school and make a checklist of all the things that needed to be done in the house that day: the laundry, washing up, paying the bills, doing the shopping, vacuuming or ironing. They were simple things that went on in every household in Britain every day, but for me they all took an enormous effort. I didn't always get through my lists at first, as I was still finding it very hard to motivate myself, but even if I only managed two or three things out of five it was better than nothing. Before, if something wasn't done by the time I fetched Charlotte at 3 p.m. then it wasn't done at all. But I started to take the view that even if it took me three hours to work up to doing the shopping and I didn't get to Sainsbury's until 6 p.m., it was still worthwhile. Seeing that I was making an effort, the children also tried to help out, running the vacuum cleaner around or going to the shops with me.

Gradually the house started to change, to brighten in mood. The dark cloud didn't exactly go, but it certainly began to lift, and we could all feel the difference. For me and the children it was a big relief, but for Mike it was very hard, seeing things change for the better in his absence. It was almost as if as soon as he went everything got better; I got better. When he came over to visit the children I might be cooking or doing some laundry and he would look at me and say, frustrated, 'See, it's not so hard, is it? Why couldn't you have done this while I was here?'

In the early days after we first split, we would often end up rowing, as Mike felt I was doing better without him than he was without me and the children. Sometimes we would talk for hours on the phone late at night, and he would plead, 'I just want to know where I stand with you. If you're happier without me, then just say. Divorce me.'

But that's not what I wanted. Yes, I was happier than I had been, but that didn't mean I wanted to slam the door shut on our marriage for ever. In many ways it would have been easier for us both if I could have said that I never wanted him back. But I couldn't say that. I didn't know when – if ever – I would want us to live as husband and wife again, but I couldn't rule it out either. So I would tell him, 'I don't want a divorce. I just want some time. Then we'll see where we are.'

Before we could even think about trying to build bridges there was still a lot for us to sort out for ourselves. We had had problems before Sarah's murder, but we had always been able to deal with them. Afterwards, our grief magnified these problems until they were simply unmanageable. Mike's temper and depression, which he had always been able to keep a lid on, spiralled out of control and started to scare me. Likewise, my tendency to keep things to myself and withdraw emotionally had alienated Mike. He wanted me to rage against Roy Whiting, like him, but I couldn't. If I ever felt myself start to lose my temper I would pull back; perhaps I thought if I started I would never stop. But I had started to realise that it was not a healthy way to live and I needed to learn how to put my feelings into words and be open and honest with Mike. But these things don't happen overnight. I needed time to do it slowly, alone.

Sarah's murder had shaken our very beings. We used to like ourselves, and be happy with the kind of people we were. But after Sarah's murder the guilt and anger had made us question everything. If we had been 'proper parents', like your average Mr and Mrs Jones, would Sarah have been killed? On the rare occasions that we received nasty letters asking us, 'What were you thinking leaving the children like that?', we would torture ourselves with it. In the months after Sarah's death we told ourselves that we should make an effort to be a more 'average' family, to have stricter rules and a less relaxed attitude. But in trying to be people that we weren't, we lost ourselves, and we had to find out who we were again.

On the one hand, Mike understood this, but the uncertainty of the situation was very hard for him, as he has always been a more black-and-white person than me. Particularly since Sarah's murder, he had found it very difficult to go with the flow, and liked things to be set out clearly. Now he felt that he was being asked to put his life on hold, without any guarantee that things would work out in the future. I know that it was unfair of me to expect that of him, but I was so scared of losing him for good. I would lie awake at night, wondering what he was doing and who he was with, and whether he might find himself a life that was easier without me in it, where there weren't the constant fights and problems. If he met somebody else it would be terrible, but the *most* terrible thing would be that I would only have myself to blame.

As the autumn set in, things started to slowly improve when Mike came round and we fought less. We weren't ready to address any big issues between us and I still couldn't fully open up to him about how I was feeling, but we were communicating better, starting to deal with the day-to-day issues. We had barely talked about the arrival of the new baby since Mike had left, but I knew it must be very hard for him to see my pregnancy progressing without him being part of it. As time went by the situation got harder and harder to ignore as every time he came round I was a little bit bigger.

One day in September when he came over to see Charlotte, and I was making us a cup of tea in the kitchen, I suddenly jumped and put my hand to my belly.

'Are you OK?' asked Mike.

'I'm fine. She's just giving me a good kicking,' I joked.

Then there was silence for a moment as it dawned on both of us that Mike had never felt his daughter kick. With my other pregnancies we had lain in bed at night, taking it in turns to watch and feel the movement.

'Can I feel?' he asked.

I took his hand and guided it to my stomach and watched his face light up as he felt our daughter's kicks. With his hand holding my belly, for a moment it was like nothing had changed between us and I hoped that, one day, we would be able to work things out and get our marriage back on track. I had always assumed that Mike and I would grow old together and I still wanted that more than anything.

13

MOTHERHOOD

On the morning of Charlotte's ninth birthday, 28 November 2003, the baby was already eight days overdue, following in the family tradition of being late. After months of discomfort, I was desperate to go into labour, but Charlotte was insisting I hold off.

'I don't want the baby to be born on my birthday,' she said moodily, arms crossed.

'Wouldn't it be fun to share your birthday with your little sister?' I asked.

'No. If the baby comes today we'll have to lie to her and pretend she was born tomorrow,' she firmly announced to the family.

After I picked Charlotte up from school that afternoon, and we had a birthday tea for her and her friends, I kept catching her looking at me anxiously and I couldn't help laughing. Luckily for her, the baby wasn't ready to put in an appearance just yet and Charlotte went to bed happy that night.

The next morning she chattered away excitedly as I took her over to a friend's house. I had been reluctant to let her stay over night with her pals after Sarah's death, but I had finally relented and agreed to a sleep over. I knew I couldn't keep her at home wrapped in cotton wool for ever and now that she had turned nine – finally older than Sarah was when she was murdered – it seemed a natural time to grant her more freedom. I headed home after dropping Charlotte and, tired from the walk, put my feet up and watched some television for a while. Lee and Luke were out playing with their mates, and it was nice to have some quiet time to myself. After a good rest, I decided to tackle a few household chores before Mike came over. Over the past weeks he had been visiting regularly, making sure that I was looking after myself, as well as helping around the house and with the children.

I was washing up when the first pain hit me at four o'clock. Taking a deep breath, I put my hand to my stomach. I'm not sure whether it was because I was older or due to the miscarriage, but my body had not coped as well with pregnancy as it had in the past. From around the seven-month mark, I had suffered from terrible stomach pains that frequently laid me up in bed. My midwife assured me that there was nothing to worry about, but it was unpleasant and anxious-making all the same. After a minute, however, the pain passed, and I carried on with the dishes. With the baby due at any time there was no way of knowing yet if it had been a 'practise pain' or the real thing.

Despite being alone in the house, I was perfectly calm. After four quick, easy labours I was confident that there would be no complications. With this in mind, I had opted to have a home birth. I had never felt comfortable giving birth in hospital. Being hooked up to machines and pumped full of drugs, with doctors and nurses rushing around in surgical scrubs, makes you feel like you are ill when actually the opposite is true: having a baby is the most natural process in the world. I had wanted to deliver my other children at home – like my mum had me – but it was usually discouraged by doctors back then. This time round, however, my midwife thought it was a great idea and I hoped that this labour would be relaxed and straightforward.

Of course, there was also another consideration. After we made the news of my pregnancy public I had received many requests from the press for interviews and pictures after the baby was born. I had decided, again, to do one exclusive piece with the *News of the World* and leave it at that. It wouldn't be fair to keep thrusting my little girl into the limelight when she had no choice about it. When she was old enough, she could make up her own mind about the issue. Yet although I told the press of my intentions regarding the baby, that didn't stop them ringing or knocking on the door. And I had no doubt that there would be photographers door-stepping the house around the date the baby was due, waiting to snap pictures of my new daughter. The decision to have her at home took these fears away. I wouldn't have to take her out into the world until I was ready.

An hour or so after the first pain, I had another strong twinge, and I started to think that my daughter might really be on her way. Just as it was passing, Mike arrived at the door.

'Any sign of her yet?' he asked with a smile.

'Actually I have had a couple of contractions.'

'How far apart?'

'An hour.'

'No rush then, is there? Sit down and I'll make you a cup of tea and we'll see how it goes.'

For the rest of the afternoon we sat together on the sofa, drinking tea, watching television and chatting companionably. The contractions kept coming, hitting me at irregular intervals, and when they struck I got up and walked around the room until they passed. At some point, the boys drifted in with their friends and we warned them that the baby was on its way. They looked slightly alarmed, no doubt expecting screaming and shouting and blood everywhere, and after a while their friends shuffled off. I had promised to call Charlotte if the baby was coming, which I did, but she decided to stay at her friends as planned, as I think she was a bit nervous about the birth.

At around nine o'clock the contractions started coming stronger and more regularly and I knew it was time to call the midwives. At a home birth there have to be two on hand, one for the baby and one for the mother. After they had arrived and established that the baby was on its way, they asked,

'Would you like to go up to the bedroom now or stay down here? We could prop you up on some pillows on the floor if you like. Wherever you'd be more comfortable.'

'I'll stay here for a while,' I said, before doubling over with a contraction and changing my mind. 'On second thoughts, perhaps we'd better go up.'

As I walked up the stairs, hand on my belly, I reflected on how relaxed the whole experience was. My mind flashed back to Sarah's birth, with the walk to Mum's with Lee and Luke followed by the nightmarish ambulance ride to the hospital, siren wailing and blue lights flashing. It seemed such a waste of time, considering that Sarah had been delivered with no problems, just minutes after getting to St Peter's. It was so nice not to have to go through that again. Once upstairs, I simply positioned myself comfortably on the bed and started to push with the aid of just a little gas and air. Mike held my hand, encouraging me every step of the way, and I was so glad that he was there. We had talked over whether he would be present at the birth and I had left the decision up to him. As far as he was concerned there was no choice to make. It was his daughter and he wanted to be at her birth. He didn't have to wait long. Just ten minutes later, our daughter was born.

Unlike in hospitals, where they whisk your baby away to be cleaned and wrapped, she was handed straight to me. I gazed down at my daughter, taking in her dark hair and eyes, and healthy complexion. We had feared that she might be on the small side, as my bump had never been very big, but she was a robust 7lb 14oz. Looking at my perfect newborn little girl, I couldn't stop the tears coming. As I sobbed, Mike lifted her slowly out of my arms and held her close, kissing her head softly, a beaming smile on his face the whole time. When I had regained my composure he passed her back, went out into the hall and called down to the boys. It had all been such a calm affair that they hadn't even realised their sister had been born and they bounded up the stairs to meet her.

Later, after the midwives left, I gave my baby her first bottle – which she took to straight away – and put her to sleep in a cot by the bed. Even at that early stage I could tell that she was going to be a good baby. I had worried that the stress of my pregnancy, with the split with Mike and the miscarriage, might affect her in a negative way. But as she settled without complaining, I felt at ease. After she was down, Mike and I stayed up chatting quietly and drinking yet more cups of tea, lying together on the bed. Far from feeling exhausted, I was on a high, and we stayed up most of the night, just watching our little girl sleep.

The next day there was one question on everyone's lips: What are you going to call her? But, like with Sarah, we had some problems deciding on a name. All through my pregnancy we had liked Lily Rose, but as with the other children, the name we had chosen in advance was not quite right. She simply wasn't a Lily. I lost count of the number of times people asked me if we were going to call her Sarah, after her sister. But that was never something we considered for a moment. I do believe in reincarnation but I never believed that my new baby actually *was*

225

Sarah. Nor was she a replacement for Sarah, she was her own person. Giving her Sarah's name would take away her identity and force her to live in her sister's shadow, something we had vowed not to let happen.

In the days after her birth, we spent hours sitting around with the family batting hundreds of names about, but none of them seemed quite right. On one occasion, Mum, Jenny, and my sister Maria were round. Brandishing a bunch of flowers that she had bought over, Mum turned to Maria and said: 'Can you put these in a vase please?'

Taking the flowers, Maria joked, 'I'm not bloody Doris you know,' referring

to a maid she had employed when she lived in South Africa. 'Doris!' I said, 'I quite like that . . .'

'We can't call her Doris, Mummy,' piped up Charlotte, 'she'll be very angry with us when she's older.'

Mike agreed, but although we decided not to call her Doris officially, the nickname stuck, just like Princess had done with Sarah. A few days later I picked up the phone and it was Mike. 'Ellie Jane Louise,' he said, without preamble. I didn't even need to think about it. 'Perfect,' I told him, and that was that.

Naming his daughter was very important to Mike. With the situation between us, it would have been easy for him to feel sidelined, which was the last thing I wanted. Whatever happened with our marriage, I wanted him to be as much a part of Ellie's life as he was the other children's when they were growing up. When everyone commented that Ellie took after Mike, I could see him swell with pride. A friend said to me years ago that all newborns look most like their dads as it is nature's way of making them bond. Mike seemed to be having no problems there, as he plainly adored his new daughter.

During my pregnancy I had worried that Ellie might be the spitting image of Sarah, but my fears turned out to be unfounded. As well as the similarities to Mike, I could see bits of all the children's looks and characteristics in her. She had Charlotte's smile, she looked like Lee when she stretched, like Luke when she fed, and when she slept she looked like Sarah. I made sure that Ellie had something in her crib from each of her brothers and sisters. She had Luke's safety blanket, a teddy bear that Lee had bought for me, a teddy of Charlotte's and Sarah's red and black shawl that I had slept with since her death. Although the shawl was well worn, Ellie loved it, seemingly attracted to the strong colours. When I woke in the night and looked over at her sleeping she would invariably have it twisted around her fingers and partially covering her face – just as her big sister had slept. Sometimes I had to look twice to make sure that it wasn't Sarah.

For the first few weeks after my daughter's birth, I cried every day. It would have been easy to blame it on my post-natal hormonal body, but the truth is that every time I looked at Ellie I was overwhelmed by memories of Sarah and couldn't stop myself bursting into tears. The memories weren't of Sarah's death, but of the real, living Sarah as she had been as a baby. The images were so strong and poignant that it bought the loss of Sarah into sharper focus and made me miss her even more. For the first time since her death I felt as if I was really grieving for her, allowing myself to feel the emotions that I had shut out for so long. After a good cry I usually felt better, cleansed, until some little thing set me off again.

From the day Ellie was born we have talked to her openly about Sarah. We have never done it in a morbid way or talked of her murder, we have simply spoken about what she was like in life. Sometimes in the daytime while Ellie has been awake I have hooked a picture of Sarah in a brass frame over the bumper of her cot so she can look at her. I feel it is important for Ellie to grow up knowing all about her big sister in a natural way. At some point in the future we know that she'll want to hear all the details of what happened, and when that time comes we will tell her everything and show her the newspaper articles. But while she is still small it is enough for her to know that she has two sisters, one just isn't around any more.

Had Sarah still been with us, I know that she would have been like a second mum to Ellie, just as she was to Charlotte as a baby, as she was always so maternal and loved looking after people. Charlotte was different. Although she can't wait to get home from school to see Ellie, she takes more of a traditional big sister role. She adores playing with her, but doesn't want to be involved with the less glamorous jobs like feeding or changing. Poignantly, she has developed a protective streak towards her little sister, making sure that everyone who holds her supports her head properly and observes other safety procedures for new babies. As the youngest, Charlotte had always been looked after by the whole family, but now she has someone smaller and more vulnerable than her who needed caring for.

We didn't take Ellie out of the house for ten days, wanting to keep her all to ourselves, but when we did Charlotte insisted that we put a clear rain hood over her pram. This meant that people could look at her, but not actually touch her. When people in the village did approach us to have a peak at our new arrival, Charlotte would start to whinge and pull on my arm, trying to drag me off. When we finally got away, she would say crossly, 'Why do *those women* want to see her?' I laughed, but part of me felt the same. Although it is perfectly natural for people to coo over newborn babies, I felt uncomfortable about it because of all we had been through. After Sarah's death I felt as if she became public property, with strangers weeping over her while even I couldn't. I didn't want the same thing to happen with Ellie. I wanted to keep her as ours and ours alone.

I had worried that the age gap between Ellie and the others would be a problem, but if anything, it has worked to our advantage. The age difference not only means that there are no jealousies over the new arrival, but also that I have my own little band of helpers. The boys were confident with their new sister from the start, holding, changing and feeding her. Lee even went out and bought her some new outfits to wear. It's almost like she has five parents, instead of two. Yet despite all the help and support the children are providing, I'm still reluctant to let Ellie far from my sight. At the end of the day I feel that I have to be the one with sole responsibility for her safety, so that if anything bad happens I will ultimately be the only one to blame.

Ellie's birth has forced me into a new daily routine, which is good for me, as I have always coped better when I am busy. Like all babies she wakes several times in the night and, as I did with Sarah, I take her into my bed to feed or simply lull her back to sleep. By five or six in the morning she is wide awake and we both rise for the day. Then there is the daily rush to get the other children ready and do the school run. After Ellie and I drop Charlotte off, Jenny usually comes back for a cup of coffee and a chat before she starts work. Often, on our return, we find cards or letters of congratulation waiting on the front mat, from well-wishers, some of whom are friends and some strangers. One family wrote to say that they had called their newborn daughter Sarah, which I was touched by, and there was even a card from Home Secretary David Blunkett, which I thought was thoughtful of him.

After Jenny leaves I have no time to sit around feeling depressed as there is always something to do for Ellie: feeding, changing and keeping her entertained, as well as making sure the house is clean for her. I've gone from spending all day every day on my own with not enough to occupy my time, to being constantly on the go.

Soon after Ellie's arrival, there was also Christmas to think about. I hadn't really enjoyed a Christmas since Sarah's death – I had simply gone through the motions for the children – but it was Ellie's first Christmas and I wanted to make it nice for her. When the children broke up from school we decorated the house, got a tree, and shopped together for presents and food. Mike came and stayed at the house for a few days, which the children were thrilled by, and there was a general spirit of celebration and good cheer that had been absent for a long time. Christmas Day was only slightly marred by Charlotte being poorly in bed, which stopped us visiting Sarah's grave for the first year since her death.

Among the other positives of Ellie's birth, it has made Mike and I take a step back and look at the way we were living before, with the stress and the constant arguments. Now, the fights that had become part of our daily lives have stopped, as we have more important things to worry about. However else we have failed together, we have always been good parents and we are determined that we will be again. Mike comes round every day without fail to spend time with us and help out, doing some jobs around the house or taking us shopping. He even stays the night occasionally, getting up at unsociable hours to feed Ellie and give me a rest. Whereas before he was spending most of his time in the pub, Mike now has a new lease of life, his depression has lifted and he has started looking for work again.

We've talked about getting back together but, being sensible for once, we know that however well we are getting on, there is still a lot of work to do on our marriage that can't be achieved overnight. Having a new baby has brought us closer together and made us feel like a proper family again, but it isn't a good enough reason in itself to get back together. We know that we have to take it one step at a time and be patient. If we were to jump in too soon it would just be a matter of time before our old problems came back to haunt us.

People always say that you should 'live for today', but I have learned through bitter experience that it is not a healthy way to exist. After Sarah's death I lived day-to-day, never looking forward, and it nearly broke me. When you live like that you give up your future and nothing really matters. Ellie's birth has reminded me that there is something to live for. She has given me back tomorrow. I'm not saying that I have found closure. If there's one thing I now know it's that there is no such thing. It is just an abstract concept that people talk about because they want to believe that the pain will come to an end. But the pain never stops and it never will. There is no point fighting against it, you just have to learn to accept it and incorporate it into your life. I will always have five children and one of them will always be an eight-year-old girl, but I can't spend my every waking hour mourning for Sarah. I still love and miss her like crazy but I have finally accepted that she is never coming back. With this acceptance, the darkness that engulfed me for so long has finally given way to some light.